A YEAR WITH
MINECRAFT

BEHIND THE SCENES AT
MOJANG

THOMAS ARNROTH

ecw press

LIBRARY AND ARCHIVES CANADA
CATALOGUING IN PUBLICATION

Arnroth, Thomas, author
Year with Minecraft : behind the scenes
at Mojang / Thomas Arnroth.

ISBN 978-1-77041-219-4

1. Persson, Markus, 1979-. 2. Mojang AB.
3. Minecraft (Game). I. Title.

HD9993.E454M63 2014
338.7'617948092   C2013-908077-5

Photos: Thomas Arnroth
Editor: Mattias Johnsson
Cover and type: Troy Cunningham
Printing: United Graphics 5 4 3 2 1
PRINTED AND BOUND IN THE UNITED STATES

MINECRAFTIA FONT © ANDREW TYLER
(WWW.ANDREWTYLER.NET)
MINECRAFTER 3 FONT © "ASHERZ08,"
"MADPIXEL," "ASHLEY DENHAM"

Copyright © 2014 Thomas Arnroth
and Paradox Interactive AB

Published by ECW Press
2120 Queen Street East, Suite 200, Toronto,
Ontario, Canada M4E 1E2
416-694-3348 / info@ecwpress.com

A YEAR WITH
MINECRAFT

1
A VISIT TO
THE RESEARCH
CENTER

Making a mistake is not an option. Jens Bergensten is like a Zen master, totally focused on the task at hand. Later, during the evening, millions of fans and gamers will have the opportunity to judge his work. And Jens, or Jeb as he is known, is not a man who leaves anything to chance. Jeb also has over 850,000 Twitter followers and is the lead game developer of Minecraft, a game with roughly 50 million players. To say that everyone's eyes are watching him is an understatement.

This simply must turn out well. Jens has made holes in a gingerbread man's head, just about where the eyes should be, a task that demanded precision and delicate hands. Now he is trying to add the last and oh-so-important detail, and as a game developer Jens knows how important a thing like this is for gamers — we are talking laser beams radiating from the cookie's eyes! Or, in this case, pink straws stuck through gingerbread. Such things are important, and Jens is not happy.

"No, this doesn't work very well," he says with his usual composure.

The schedule is tight. There is only one hour left until the day's work will be made public. But unlike any other day, Jens has a whole team working with him. There are six people crowded in the room together, and the person with the main responsibility is Markus Persson, or Notch, as his 1.4 million Twitter followers call him. He is the one who created Minecraft in the spring of 2009. In late 2011, he considered himself done with it and officially handed over the responsibility to Jens. Notch moved onto develop a new game, a space adventure that by his standards is enormous. But at the moment he is busy with a side project on which both he and Jens are doing their utmost.

It is a Friday afternoon in December 2012. And on Friday afternoons, you play games. That is, if you work at the game developing studio Mojang. We are in a part of Stockholm called Söder, which translates to something like Southside or the South, in an office space that was recently voted Sweden's most stylish. Mojang and its 26 employees are having their scheduled game day. Although "play day" might be a better label on this particular day, because it is neither video games nor board games they are engaging

Markus Persson helps light the photo of the two surviving gingerbread houses, while Lydia Winters fixes the black backdrop.

in. Instead they are having a hard fought competition of building the best, most impressive Mojang-inspired gingerbread house. It is a messy scene, but who cares about that when the cleaners are in on a daily basis?

However, Markus Persson does not agree on the term "playing games"; he does not even want to call it play. To him, it is research. No wonder Lydia Winters, with the fascinating job title director of fun, tweets: "Mojang = Best ever." On the other hand, she only does that after the following Monday's snowball fight. Indoors that is.

Jens is right though. His laser beams don't turn out well

at all, they simply look like pink straws stuck through a man-shaped cookie. Not very creepy and, hence, not to be included in the final creation — a gingerbread robot going berserk amongst a crowd of gingerbread men, complete with blood and ripped off heads.

I have scheduled an interview with Markus that is supposed to take a half hour. While he is melting sugar, the glue to paste gingerbread pieces together, I ask him if he has time for it. Hmm, he answers, a short one then, it's bad timing, you know. The gingerbread house and all.

Yes, I get it. The interview only lasts for five minutes. But I'm used to that. The first time I met Markus and was trying to exchange a few words, he was standing by the office pinball machine.

"Hi," I said.

"Hi, sorry, I don't have time to talk now, I'm in the middle of a game," he said.

Next time I saw him he was carrying a glass of brownish fluid, it was another Friday. I asked him if he was having a scotch.

"No, it's brandy," he said and walked past.

So five minutes is not to be frowned upon, especially on a day like this.

On this very special research day, they are divided into three teams. Markus is in charge of one. Mojang's other two founders and part owners, Jakob Porser and Carl Manneh, are in charge of the other two. Jakob and his team are aiming for a more folksy approach by transforming their precast house into a log cabin with the help of pretzel sticks and melted sugar. They give the house a fence too, made by the same sticks. Jon Kågström is the one fiddling with the fence; Jon used to work at Dice and was part of the team that made the widely popular Battlefield games.

Team Manneh is going with a Minecraft theme; they are making a green creeper, the most famous monster in the game, so famous that it has now become something of a symbol for it even though the game's main character is Steve. They have, just like Markus's team, not settled with the house's original shape; instead they have altered the pieces by sawing and cutting before applying the green color. Carl is showing an impressive ability for multi-tasking; he is supervising everything his team is doing, while at the same time spreading green icing on a piece of gingerbread.

"You can see what we're aiming for, right," he asks. It is a rhetorical question; he does not really need, or even want, an answer. He nods with satisfaction.

"Yes, you can see what we're doing, indeed."

Linn Hultman is the one who came up with the idea for the competition. She also established the rules. She is Markus's personal assistant and the office manager. But because she happens to be the office manager at Mojang, the job is a bit different than in most other places.

"It's not just that I make sure that all the practical things in the office work; I'm in charge of organizing parties and that kind of stuff too. There are quite a lot of them, this being Mojang and all. And I'm a sucker for Christmas," she says.

No one has time to get into details about the rules with me, the clock is ticking and so forth, but as far I understand, the teams have two hours to build their house. They have to base their work on the same basic materials, which in short consists of ready-made gingerbread houses. Linn provides sugar and stuff needed to make icing. They could just glue the parts together and create a standard issue house, but of course that would not do on a day like this. Everyone was informed about the event the day before and had the chance to add things to the basic materials, such as candy or cotton. But they are not allowed to use any extra special equipment. This leads to Lydia impounding her boyfriend Vu Bui's semi-professional camera. She thinks it is unfair that he will be able to take better pictures than the others. "You are not allowed to bring your own special equipment," she argues. Lydia is on Jakob's team, Vu on Carl's.

Carl and Vu glower through a window at Markus's team and point out that they have brought a glue gun from home. If that is not special equipment, then what is?

COTTON DOES INDEED BURN

I also have an appointment with Carl this afternoon. He is not trying to cancel, but points out that it will have to be short, since he needs to focus on the competition. Before we sit down, he asks the rest of his team if they all know what to do. They are all concentrating too hard on the tasks at hand to even answer him. Carl takes that as a good sign and off we go. But he is not as focused as he usually is. Normally Carl is extremely well composed, the ultimate cool CEO who rarely says something he does not mean. Now he can't stop calling every month August.

"It was in August, or no, in June I mean. That's right, we moved in August, or no, what am I saying, June. Why do I keep saying August when I mean August? What am I saying? What is it with August?"

I give up and instead we grab a beer before Carl slips back to his team. This is not going to be a day for deep and revealing interviews, I realize, and so I just start watching instead.

There is something absolutely fascinating about seeing these game developers and graphic artists competing in something so unrelated to video games as decorating ginger-bread houses. There is concentration, precision and serious construction plans. There is perfect logic and order in the chaos. They have very specific goals and clear plans. Yet, in the middle of this dead serious determination, there is a lot of play and goofing off.

When the competition is finished, the houses will be photographed and published on Mojang's website. The fans will be invited to vote over the weekend, but to prevent everyone from voting on Markus's house they will not reveal who is part of which team. Instead the teams are given the names The Ginger Heroes, Team Fully Edible and Lag Nord. The fans are encouraged to vote, but the text ends with a reservation: "Although this is incredibly serious business, the results of this competition will have no bearing on the future of Minecraft, MineCon or anything else of significance. It's just for fun."

Such things may be necessary to point out when you have such devoted fans as Mojang does.

Carl's team goes all the way with their creeper and tries to mimic what might happen in the game. In Minecraft, the green creeper places itself close to you, and then it explodes. The consequences are devastating. Most likely there is nobody who has played Minecraft who hasn't been killed by a creeper. So of course he should be on fire in real gingerbread life.

Vu is taking photos while sparklers are lit. He regained his camera from Lydia with the glue gun argument (or rather, he successfully convinced Linn, who took it from Lydia, who seemed to have forgotten all about the fun part of her job title during the competition). I had overheard a somewhat surprising argument between two of the members of Carl's team, an argument about whether cotton is flammable or not, but I had not thought much of it. These are after all some extremely smart people. But seeing that the "the cotton is not flammable" argument obviously won,

Vu Bui puts the finishing touch on the green creeper, just moments before it goes up in flames because, oh yes, cotton does burn.

I am not so sure anymore. As one could expect, it all goes wrong. Not only the cotton, but the whole creeper is set on fire. I do not see the fire in time, but hear the screams and laughter. I arrive just as Daniel Kaplan — business developer, first person hired at Mojang and in 2011 nominated as one of the world's 30 most interesting young game developers — covers the gingerbread creation with white foam from the fire extinguisher. The fire door is opened in order to ventilate the room and Carl notes quietly that it is a bit strange that the fire alarm did not go off.

It is rock and roll, game developer style.

Finally, the houses are lined up on the long rustic dinner table in the middle of the studio. Vu is going to take pictures of the two houses that have not been set ablaze (he was able to get some good ones of the creeper before it went down) and Markus adds some extra mood to it by holding two candles at a distance. There is a heated discussion between Jens, Jakob, Vu and Markus about which house should actually win.

Markus gets two glasses of tequila, one for him and one for Lydia. But Lydia does not want it right now, which makes Markus shout, "Sweet, that means I get both shots." Jakob pours himself a glass of Laphroaig. He is not planning on a late night — in 15 minutes he needs to leave the office in order to take the shuttle home to the small town of Knivsta, north of Stockholm, where his family is waiting. By now I have spent so much time with Jakob and the others that, even if I am not part of the gang, I am no stranger. But taking some of their most expensive whiskey without asking does not feel right, so I ask Jakob if it is okay.

"God yes," he says.

I laugh and shake my head a little. There is something very disarming about Jakob's manners in combination with drinking one of the world's most luxurious scotches at four o'clock in the afternoon; it feels a bit wacky. Or maybe I am just embarrassed by asking. However, Jakob notices my subtle reaction and looks worryingly at me.

"Oh, I'm sorry. I didn't mean to," he says.

I am startled; I have no clue of what he means by that; why does he apologize, I ask.

"It was stupid of me to use the God-word, I'm so sorry if I offended you," he explains.

It is rock and roll, well behaved game developer style.

OUTSIDE THE HUMBLE DOORS OF MOJANG

The gingerbread houses are built on Saint Lucia's Day, a Swedish festivity celebrated on December 13. Nearly 50,000 people vote on which house they think should win, and the winner turns out to be Markus's team.

Almost 12 months earlier, I visited Mojang for the first time. Back then they were located in a converted apartment on a backstreet called Åsögatan, maybe a 10 minute walk from their new premises where the epic gingerbread house battle was fought. This part of town, the south, used to be the working class area of Stockholm, but nowadays it is dominated by hipsters and people working in media and the gaming industry. It is the same way here as in so many other big cities in Europe; what used to be poor, working class central areas are now trendy, attracting creative businesses and people. The prices have skyrocketed.

Standing outside, one could not help but be a bit struck by the fact that behind that very modest and ordinary entrance was one of the world's hottest gaming studios. As a matter of fact, at the end of 2012, Mojang was voted the second best game studio in the world by influential game magazine *Edge*.

It was one of those boring Nordic January days without any snow or sun — not dark, but neither very bright, like the day never got started. It was gloomy, at best. The remarkable fact that behind that street door were a bunch of guys who some 15 months earlier were largely unknown, but now were pulling in hundreds of millions making video games, was reinforced by the everydayness of it all.

However, Stockholm is one of the world's leading cities when it comes to making games. In this part of the city, game developing is the number one profession. Probably Montreal is the only city in the world with more game developers per capita. Game series such as Battlefield and Just Cause are produced here, in the same neighborhood as a matter of fact.

Dice, the studio where Jon Kågström used to work, has a staff of almost 400 and makes the highly acclaimed game series Battlefield, of which Battlefield 3 (released in 2011) has sold over 20 million copies; it was just a short walk away. Avalanche, which has made a name for itself with the Just Cause games, was just two blocks away. Both of them were residing in flashier premises than Mojang.

But standing outside the door, waiting for someone to let me in, I realized that Mojang actually was situated right where Dice, Avalanche and almost all the other now well-known Swedish game developers once started, back in the '90s. In less than 10 blocks from Mojang you would find the original addresses for some 20 developers, many who still exist in one form or another, like Paradox Interactive — today one of the world's few publishing houses for strategy games. They actually started out more or less next door to Mojang; today they reside in one of the few skyscrapers on the southside — and standing on one of their balconies you could actually see the rooftop of Mojang's house. Heck, you could probably throw a stone at it, they were that close by. I realized that if, in the future, there were to be held guided historic street walking tours for gamers in Stockholm, this is where those tours would head. It would be perfect for out-of-shape gamers too, a 15 minute walk should cover it.

But in order to get a short lesson in the history of video games, one did not have to walk the streets of this area at all. Instead, one could just enter Minecraft.

THE LANGUAGE CALLED GAMING

Minecraft can sometimes appear as something completely new in the gaming industry. It is far from it.

One can rather see it as a mix-up of and a tribute to many of the most beloved games and game mechanics. The pixels and rough graphics, which have now become such a distinctive expression of Minecraft, are a homage to some of the oldest games in the short history of gaming. In reality it is derived from '80s and '90s video games. Think early Nintendo games. When I once turned Minecraft off after a longer gaming session, I happened to catch a glimpse of an old Tetris game and my first thought was that oh no, not yet another game trying to mimic Minecraft. Then I realized the absurdity of the situation; the original Tetris was made in the beginning of the '80s, right about when Markus Persson stopped wearing diapers. Yet the graphic style of Minecraft is considered so peculiar today that the Museum of Modern Art (MoMA) in New York has included the game in its new permanent game design exhibition.

Neither are the basic game mechanics in Minecraft new. Tasks like gathering food to eat or resources for construction and crafting have been seen in games since the late '80s. Gamers have done this in such well-known games as Civilization, SimCity and Age of Empires. They have carved and placed blocks in different shapes in games like Dungeon Keeper and, my personal favorite, Stronghold, just to name a few.

This is something Markus is aware of and has made no secret of. "Minecraft is like a mixture of everything I loved about games when I grew up. It's full of it," says Markus.

The point is that he has made something different with it. That is where the uniqueness and innovation lies. Or in Markus's own words:

"I try to create my own dialect of the language that's called gaming."

It is a dialect much about freedom, because that is what Markus has done so well with Minecraft: he has created a game where the players can roam free and just play around with his creation. Minecraft might be, as someone wrote, the most ugly yet beautiful game released in the last 10 years, but this does not prevent MoMA from including it in their exhibition or the famed Dungeon Keeper creator Peter Molyneux from calling it the most important game of the decade.

Markus himself has gone from being a shy nerd no one had heard of to becoming one of the gaming industry's most famous names, from being an unknown designer doing web based games that no one cared about, to being declared a genius. At the time of writing in early 2013, Minecraft has sold over 20 million copies if you count all editions of the game. If you include all pirated copies there is certainly twice, maybe even three times, as many full games circulating around the world — which is not very surprising since Markus himself basically encourages people who can't afford to buy the game to pirate it instead. They can pay later.

As fascinating as the success of the actual game is, just as exciting is the story of the man behind it. Or rather, the story of how you can become immensely rich by making a seemingly ugly game. Markus was good for tens of millions already back in early 2012; a few years from now it will most likely be hundreds of millions. In schoolyards, children are discussing their latest builds in Minecraft just as much as they talk about how Markus, or Notch as most of them call him, earned his first million. It is not only the game that attracts players; Markus does too. He has become the gaming industry's first modern superstar, an idol who makes children dream of becoming game developers. Markus is someone who proves that developing games can be its own form of rock and roll, with its own kind of stars, and fans for that matter. Where the majority of game developers remain anonymous, Notch has become synonymous with one of the world's most played games. Which is all the more odd since Markus is not very comfortable being at the center of attention; he is in fact very, very shy and reserved to the point of it being something of a problem for him.

"IT JUST TURNED OUT THAT WAY"

What made Minecraft, Markus and Mojang so big were not just the game and its creator. It was also the timing.

"Everything was in place in a way you can't fix yourself. Social media, YouTube, online payment solutions, fast broadband connections, good enough computers in many homes and almost all young kids around the globe playing games. With the right timing, Minecraft and Markus is what can happen," says Mojang's London-based lawyer Alex Chapman of Sheridans, who operates somewhere in between law and business development. Markus agrees with Chapman.

"The timing was right in so many ways. It really doesn't feel as if anything that's happened has been planned by me. I mean, how could I plan this? It only turned out this way, much to my own surprise."

Just take a thing such as YouTube, which has become so essential to the spread of Minecraft. In hindsight, YouTube was just waiting for a game like Minecraft to happen. There were already hundreds of thousands, or rather millions, of young game-loving people wanting to express themselves and their gaming through videos. Allen DeBevoise, CEO of Machinima, the largest YouTube channel focusing on videos with game content, has called them "the Lost Boys" in an *L.A. Times* interview: young men of a certain age that were largely unreached by advertising.

What was lacking was a game that allowed the Lost Boys to express themselves freely. Sure, long before Minecraft, most games gave players many opportunities to display their skills; there were many games about building and handling resources out there too. But in those cases the gamer was always limited by the design or game mechanics.

Somewhere, the game developers had always decided what could and needed to be done to succeed in the game. If it was about building things, the game decided what you could build and roughly how it would turn out. In The Sims for example, the players spend just as much time on building and designing their houses as they do controlling the characters in the game. But you cannot build anything other than houses, decorate homes and in that use things the developers have added to the game. A maypole can only be placed if it is ready-made in one of the game menus. And it can only look the way the graphic artist at the game studio designed it.

Not in Minecraft though. Do you want a maypole? All you have to do is chop down trees and gather the material you need. Do you want to build a small cave? Just chop yourself into the mountain. Want a whole cave system? Well then, just keep chopping. Oh, you would rather build a replica of the White House or the Starship *Enterprise*? Well, just do it. Someone else does not settle with that, but builds a calculator that actually works. Another player decides to recreate entire levels of other games in Minecraft. All you need is imagination, skill, patience and time.

And because what is built becomes unique, YouTube is the perfect way to show it off to others. You can even record it while you are actually building. Admittedly you build with Minecraft's help, but in a game irrefutably made by Markus Persson, you do not build his stuff — you build something that is completely unique to you. That is why you can stand inside your own game, the one you have running on your computer, Xbox 360 or iPhone, and look out over a landscape that only you and no one else in the world can see. It is your very own version of Minecraft. That is why it is so tempting to share it with others: *it is my own world, the world I built all by myself, come look!*

One of the bigger YouTube sensations during the last few years is CaptainSparklez, or Jordan Maron, which is his real name. He was reasonably popular for a couple of years when he recorded videos where he was commenting on and playing the Call of Duty games. He then switched to making Minecraft videos in late 2010 and in months more than tripled his amount of followers, from 30,000 to 100,000. In early 2011, together with a few of his friends, he had the brilliant idea of making music parodies by using Minecraft. From that moment, his life changed.

"Revenge," a parody of Usher's "DJ Got Us Fallin' in Love," has over 122 million views. His Minecraft style parody of PSY's "Gangnam Style" also has millions of views. CaptainSparklez's channel has roughly six million followers and Jordan himself has become both rich and famous in the process.

Such is the power of Minecraft.

INFRASTRUCTURE FOR THE SHY

But besides YouTube there is also the power of blogging and tweeting. For Markus that has been the key to success, the very reason for him emerging as the gaming world's most well-known person. As I have already stated, and which I think will be shown more clearly as you read this book, he is one of those quiet, shy and very reserved people, the type who becomes uncomfortable in a crowd and completely silent if they do not know almost everyone in the room. He is one of those people who is so smart that school becomes boring, one who does not care one bit about sports.

Or, once again, in Markus's own words: "Internet and social media suits people like me, we who are shy and slightly introverted. It gives us a chance to be seen. It is a space where people like me can make a place for ourselves. It gives me the opportunity to make myself heard."

And heard he is. With over 1.4 million followers on Twitter he even holds a certain power.

"But when I started writing more publicly back in 2009 it was only on my blog. It was mostly about Minecraft and the ones who read it were people I already knew, gamers and game developers from forums where I was hanging out. Then it started to grow, rather slowly in the beginning, and I sort of grew with it. Today it has become so huge; one million is a lot of followers. It would've been very difficult if it all had started that big. I truly don't know if that would've worked for me."

Then there was the thing about broadband, computers and payment solutions. Fast broadband makes it easy to download Minecraft, and sufficient broadband is available almost everywhere (or at least where Minecraft's potential costumers reside). The game is complex and big, but not as demanding for the computer as many other games out there. For example, before you buy the latest Battlefield or Call of Duty game, you better check up on the specifications needed from the computer to even run the game. Not with Minecraft. If you have a reasonably new and well-functioning computer, you are probably good to go. You simply do not need an advanced gaming computer in order to play, and since good enough broadband is common enough in most countries you are all set up.

Not very long ago, the systems and solutions for online payment were complicated and expensive. By 2009, however, anyone could use very simple standard solutions to charge customers on a website.

THE MAIN CHARACTER

So there you have him, the unexpected and unlikely idol and multimillionaire. Markus Persson, alias Notch, thin haired and not the fittest in the crowd. With a trademark fedora hat, he is well mannered, polite and principled. Happy, kind and talkative after a few drinks and who, before going to a party, tweets, "when I go out for the night, I still try to be polite." He had the whole world at his feet, flew in private jets, gave away millions to his employees and rented Stockholm's flashiest nightclub for his birthday party. What did he do next? Well, he started building an entirely new game, a space game where everyone should be able to have their own spacecraft with programmable on-board computers. He walked around with a big smile on his face at parties, not so much because he had had a shot of tequila or two, but because he was in the flow of coding or just happy that he solved a certain problem in the game mechanics, explaining such things as convex shapes not being a problem but concave ones, on the other hand, being significantly harder. When going to Thailand for holiday with his mother, sister and her daughter over Christmas, he sits by the pool and plays with a new programming language because he gets "so incredibly bored" if he "drops everything."

Perhaps Mojang's modest front door on the unremarkable street was rather fitting after all?

"Look," says Markus, "the truth of it is that I love making games. I love coding. No matter how rich I get, no matter how much money I seem to have and all the things I could do with it, the bottom line is that coding and making games is the funnest thing I can imagine."

2
HOW WOULD YOU LIKE WORKING AT MOJANG?

Upon my first visit to Mojang in early 2012 the entire office was empty. It was just after New Year's and I guessed the Mojangstas, as Markus calls the employees at Mojang, needed a break. There were no gingerbread houses to be seen; then again, this was 10 months before Linn was even hired. There were not even any children ringing at the front door, something that otherwise happened quite regularly — young fans who somehow managed to get through the street door down in the hallway and then knocked at Mojang's door with excitement in their eyes. They were often rewarded with a foam pickaxe or at least an autograph.

So it was just me and Daniel Kaplan in the office. Daniel is a man who always seems to be at ease. At times he might appear a bit absent-minded, but I suspect that is mostly because he does not easily get stressed. When we met that day he had just made the "30 Under 30" list and been named one of the gaming industry's most interesting people under 30 by *Develop*, probably the world's most prestigious magazine for game developers.

"It's nice to be appreciated, and it's a good feeling to know that someone in the industry out there actually knows I exist. But I'm no fool, I understand that I'm not on that list for anything I've actually done; it's Minecraft's glory reflected upon me. That's okay though, I'm fine with that. It's still very nice," said Daniel.

In early 2012, 17 people were working at Mojang. Not everyone had their workspace at Åsögatan yet, and during the spring more people would be hired. In January and February one of the rooms was still used as a game room. In March, the game room was gone and instead there were desks and chairs there.

Markus was nowhere to be seen.

"He is almost never here these days. He's at home, coding," said Daniel.

Markus had good reasons for staying home; it was crowded, the air was bad, there were journalists like me threateningly waiting in the office and, to add to it, there was only the one bathroom. Converting a flat from the early 1900s to a modern office had its downside.

Daniel was the first to be hired by Mojang. He had the job title business developer, but that role was now changing.

When Daniel Kaplan first tried out Minecraft in 2009, he thought the design was crap. That didn't stop him from becoming the first one employed by Mojang in October 2010.

He was on his way to being in charge of bringing Mojang's games to new platforms. In other words, taking Minecraft from the computer to, for example, another gaming console. In that role, he was more of a producer than a business developer really. And it was producing he was doing that day in January 2012. Minecraft was going to migrate from the computer to Microsoft's Xbox 360 gaming console, a not entirely uncomplicated story. Daniel was trying out an early version of the game.

"It will be slightly different than the original Minecraft," he explained. "Console players are not the same breed as those who play on the computer. You have to explain more, the tutorials in the game must be clearer. That is kind of expected when you play console games."

Not only kids, but also the occasional parent had started appearing at the apartment door. Once there was a very tired mother who wondered if they please, please, please could make it easier for her children to play Minecraft online with their friends. She was tired of having to act like some kind of IT engineer to set up a server herself, on top of hearing her kids talk about Minecraft day in and day out.

In Minecraft for Xbox 360, there would be no problem with online gaming. There you would be able to play with other Xbox players online. You would also be able to play up to four persons on the same TV screen. However, instead of being made in Stockholm, the Scottish 4J Studios in Dundee was developing the game. Kaplan was leading the production at a distance.

"The Xbox edition will always be based on an old version of the original, that is, Minecraft as a computer game. I suspect that it will probably always be at least a year behind in development. That is why we can hand over the development to someone else. 4J are not really adding new things, they are only adapting it to a different platform and a different way of controlling the game. It's not an easy task and they are much better at that than we are," explained Daniel.

It may not sound so strange when you think about it. To the contrary, it is smart. Bringing in a small subcontractor for the job you do not want to or cannot do yourself is just bona fide entrepreneurship. But for a small indie studio like Mojang to do that? It is almost as if an artist would let someone else mass-produce their own work and then exhibit it. Or maybe as if a rock group had another group record covers close to their relatively old original songs and then release them under the original band's name.

It is not a perfect comparison of course, but indie game developers are a bit like the artists of the gaming industry. They pride themselves in craftsmanship and usually do not make games with the sole purpose of selling them; it is much more a question of making games that are important to the developers themselves. Seldom, or never, do they outsource the construction of the game. And even if they would want to, few, if any, can afford to.

So in early 2012 it was obvious that Mojang was in a stage where they were growing from being just a small, if extremely hip, studio that only made the one game, to becoming more of a regular business. Because in hiring 4J Studios they were actually acting as larger, more corporate studios and video game companies often do. There was nothing wrong with that, of course; it was just not your typical indie developer move.

During the first months of 2012, there were a lot of practical things that needed to be resolved: Mojang needed a system in place to give support to the then five million players that had bought the game. If you had a question or a problem with Minecraft, you had to wait at least several weeks for an answer, if you even got one. Mojang also had to move to new premises. They had to make it easier to play Minecraft online; having tired mothers turning up at the door was a sign as good as any that the issue needed some attention. And they also wanted to act as a publisher for other, less fortunate indie developers. The latter would partly be solved by moving to new and larger premises. At least that was the plan that gray day in January 2012.

"We're growing fast, it feels like maybe too fast," said Daniel. "But what else can we do? There are some practical consequences from having as many players as we do on Minecraft. We need to be able to take care of all our gamers in a good way, it's really a responsibility, you know."

In the new premises, Mojang would come to have more workstations than employees, the thought being that other indie developers could use those empty seats. There had even been plans on buying a house down the street. But the house turned out to be badly damaged by water, so owning and managing their own property quickly became less attractive of an idea. But the dream to help other, smaller developers lived on.

"The idea is that we will be publishing their games, and that they will be able to develop the games sitting very close to all of us. Then we can help them with the developing and it gets easier for them to publish their games. We have millions of fans we can market new games to," said Daniel.

THE MAN IN RED

It was also at Åsögatan I met Jens "Jeb" Bergensten for the first time. He was 32 years old, to become 33 in a few months, his birthday being in May, a few weeks before Markus's. Something Jens likes to point out: he may not be richer than Markus, but he certainly is older. He is tall, skinny and wears his long red hair in a ponytail. He also has an equally red beard.

When we met in early spring 2012, Mojang had just hired a few people in the U.S. who would start managing the customer services and help desk. Later during the year, a Swedish support team would be added. This was a huge relief for both Jens's conscience and his inbox. When we met he had just recently been able to empty it of all the emails concerning support issues that he was supposed to take care of. It was over 100,000 emails. But, as Jens pointed out, no way could he both develop Minecraft and at the same time answer that many questions concerning the players' problems. No matter how much he wanted to.

Jens was the second person hired by Mojang. Furthermore, he was also one of the first people in the world to play Minecraft. He got it online from Markus in the spring of 2009, a few months before it was released to the general public.

"I played it with a friend for several days straight. I remember that I built many pyramids. Looking back at it, it's strange that I didn't realize that Minecraft would become so huge; I mean we were instantly hooked. But no, I didn't realize it, not at all," he says.

A couple of months later, Markus and Jens met in person for the first time. It was in July when a few hundred Swedish indie developers met for their own small festival called No More Sweden in Skövde, Daniel Kaplan's hometown. Daniel was also there.

"I didn't know Markus before then, but he had already started to become famous in our circles. Minecraft was out and we knew it had sold pretty well, at least compared to what we were used to. Besides, many of us had already tried the game and liked it," says Jens.

Jens also remembers a strange notion he had; he wanted to help Markus with the game.

"But I thought that he probably wanted to make his game by himself. That's how it is with us indie developers, we make our games by ourselves because we want to make the games we dream of. Not anyone else's game. Still, I wanted to help him. But when I talked to him about Minecraft, it also turned out that he wanted to expand it to an adventure with monsters and all. I didn't think that

Jens Bergensten is ready to fight with a foam sword, in front of the wall at Mojang's office that was painted with a large Minecraft-inspired scene.

was a good plan at all. I had played the game as a sandbox game, almost a construction kit, and that was my image of it. I didn't agree with him."

THE DIFFICULTY OF BEING INDIE

When they met, Jens was already a seasoned programmer. He had worked as a consultant at many well-known Swedish game studios. Among other things he had been involved in making Knights of the Temple for Starbreeze and the infamous Valhalla Chronicles for Oblivion, a game studio that no longer exists but had its office almost next door to Mojang's at Åsögatan. Valhalla Chronicles was barely finished when it was released in 2003, and got the following review from the website GameSpot: "Valhalla Chronicles is so dumbed down that it's practically an insult to anyone who can walk and chew gum at the same time."

Well, it was not exactly Jens's fault. It did however make him realize that making games was his calling. Not only that; he knew he wanted to make games in a particular way.

"I really didn't mind working with a lot of people at bigger productions. But what I didn't like was that no one listened to my ideas," he says.

It was his experiences at Starbreeze and Oblivion that led him to the indie scene.

"I liked how the indie scene thought when it came to video games, about making games alone or in small groups and only in the way you yourself wanted," he says.

But he also realized that he needed to become a better programmer in order to succeed. Being good at only one or a few things was not enough; you had to know a little bit about everything if you wanted to make your own productions. That was why he started studying to become a civil engineer in computer science.

During his studies, he built the strategy game Harvest: Massive Encounter together with his friends Pontus Hammarberg and Daniel Brynolf. Together they formed Oxeye Game Studio. Oxeye was the only independent indie game studio that Mojang worked with when I met Daniel and Jens for the first time. Mojang acts as a publisher for their game Cobalt, a game Jens tries to find time to develop when he is not working on Minecraft during 2012. In other words, rarely.

Harvest was Cobalt's predecessor, Jens's first attempt to make a game according to his own head. When it was released in May 2008, the large website IGN gave the game a mediocre review, but there were many players who liked it a lot more and wrote their own reviews, encouraging others to ignore what IGN wrote because Harvest "is awesome." Swedish reviews were more favorable. You cannot, however, find all that many reviews of the game and it does not seem to have made a big impression, neither in the media nor in Jens's wallet. It did not exactly have bad sales, but definitely not good enough either.

"I was studying every day and working with the game every single night. At first I lived off of study loans, then after graduation I worked part-time in the mornings and the rest of the time I spent working on the game. In my opinion, Harvest was pretty good in the end. But the problem was that it didn't do well enough. It sold some, but not in a way that meant I could afford to develop another game. I couldn't really see what a future as an indie developer would look like. I wanted to make games in that personal way, but how could I make enough money to live from it? It seemed impossible at the time."

In other words: Jens, Pontus and Daniel could not live off the royalties. Far from it. The three partners had no other option but to do more consulting, both as regular programmers for IT companies and developing Facebook games for others. Until one day in the fall of 2010, when Daniel Kaplan called Jens up and asked if he wanted to come work with him at his new workplace, a game studio called Mojang that just had been founded by Markus Persson.

Suddenly things looked up. Maybe, after all, there was a solution to the problem of making games the indie way and, at the same time, making ends meet.

3
WE WON
ANOTHER
AWARD

Minecraft went from being almost unknown in 2009 to becoming an online phenomenon during 2010. A reason for that was that some influential people and websites recognized the game. One of the first major gaming sites that acknowledged Minecraft was Penny Arcade, whose founders also started the game conventions PAX Prime and PAX East, America's two largest game conventions for consumers. But perhaps even more important was that the game developers at Valve blogged about Minecraft.

Valve is the studio behind games like Counter-Strike, Half-Life and Markus's favorite game, Team Fortress 2. (And here is a tip: if you see someone called Notch wearing a hat in TF2, then it is probably Markus playing and wearing the special hat that Valve made for him.) They also own Steam, the world's leading site for the digital sale of games. Last but not least, Valve is one of the world's most prestigious game companies; completely independent from the major game publishers, it is probably the most prestigious working place in the world for a game developer. When, for example, what was said to be an example of Valve's handbook for new employees was leaked to the press it was big news in the gaming world.

Minecraft sales increased drastically when the Valve developers blogged about the game, but for Markus the recognition from some of his favorite developers was equally important.

That fall, in September 2010, I had my first interview with him shortly after he had visited Valve himself. It turned out that they had had ulterior motives with the blog posts: they wanted to come in contact with Markus so that they could try to recruit him. It was, to say the least, flattering. He was flown to Seattle in first class, stayed in a very nice room at a luxury hotel and had a meeting with Valve where they praised his game and tested his qualities as a programmer.

"It was great to be there, to sit with Valve and know they found me interesting enough to recruit. That was really awesome, of course. But at the same time, they weren't entirely positive. They had a lot of nice things to say about my way of programming and solving problems, but they also said that I had a hard time working in a group and was

When Notch and Jeb get on stage at MineCon 2012, they are greeted as rock stars by 7,000 fans.

not that good at collaborating with others. It was a form of reality check, but on the other hand they were probably right. I do like to work alone," Markus says.

THE FIRST INTERVIEW

My interview with him was the first interview he did in Sweden, probably one of the first in the world he did with traditional media. The following article was published in late September 2010 with the headline "Sweden's unknown gaming millionaire":

Minecraft is currently offline. The server has simply crashed because of the large amount of people wanting to buy the game. That's what happens when you suddenly become as successful as Markus Persson.

After developing small games in Flash for nearly five years, last year Markus decided to concentrate on his own, slightly bigger game. He launched a first version of Minecraft in June, started working part-time as a web developer and nurtured a dream of one day being able to pull in a decent full-time salary.

Almost a year later, he has sold games for roughly 16 million Swedish crowns [note: that is about $2.4 million U.S.]. He sells them himself, through his now crashed website. There are no middlemen other than the one who sells the payment solution. Minecraft has become a global success.

"Everything feels surreal. I did think that I would be able to live off the game, but not that I would become rich," he says.

Markus currently has some problems along the lines of the crashed server. For example he has discovered that there is a limit to how much money you can transfer between bank accounts online. He has discovered that he must quickly form a limited company rather than a sole proprietor and has also an accountant who can take care of that stress.

"I haven't changed my lifestyle, but for a while I

considered investing in an apartment. Now I'm going to invest in my new company instead. Then it becomes more important to do smart things fiscally as well, I want to be able to hire whomever I want and be able to guarantee wages for a while and such things," he says.

If everything goes according to plan, Mojang AB (the name has not yet been approved) will soon exist with five or six employees and with an office in central Stockholm. Markus will continue working with Minecraft, while the other developers will take on a new game idea. Markus has also hired a business developer and is looking for a web developer.

Minecraft has been sold to nearly 160,000 people who bought it for 9.99 euros — even though it's not in its beta stage yet. When the beta is launched, hopefully before Christmas, the price will be raised to 14.99 euro and when the game is finally finished it will be 19.99 euro. Whoever catches on now will be on for the whole ride. Markus has not done any advertising for the game other than blogging about it on forums.

"The sales curve has precisely followed how active I've been with the blogging. It's probably a matter of trust; I've been very open with the users and that's probably why they also believe that I will finish the game."

[. . .] In one year, Markus has gone from being a completely unknown Flash programmer to almost a cult figure in the indie gaming world, headhunted

by some of the world's most reputed developers, and a
multimillionaire. How does that feel?

"Everything feels rather surreal. But yesterday I was
actually recognized on the subway, it was a lot of fun."

It was a strange feeling to read that article again two years after it was published, as I worked on this book in 2012. Back then, in 2010, I had never even heard of Markus before and did not know anything about Minecraft other than what I had quickly read online. I also remembered what a big surprise it was to hear about the tremendous amount of money he had earned: $2.4 million was a very large sum for anyone, especially for an indie game developer. Most other indie developers would be happy if they made ends meet and had enough to continue making games. However, in the spring of 2011, when the company made its first fiscal report for taxation, Mojang had yielded a profit of $10 million on a turnover of about $75 million. And then one should know that almost all expenses at that time, about $65 million were license fees paid straight to Markus's private company, Notch Development. In that context, $2.4 million did not sound like much anymore.

But I also remembered my thoughts after the interview, about him creating his own video game company. I thought it was very sweet of Markus to somehow give back to the indie community by hiring game developers and allowing them to make games under his wings. But I also thought it was a bit naive and that he probably would lose his money.

I guess I was wrong.

"But you weren't the only one," comforts Markus. "There were many who discouraged me. Actually, most people did."

However, it was symptomatic that my story was published at the early fall of 2010. It was, as noted, at that time that Minecraft really went from being a game in the margin to becoming famous. The story of how a singular and nerdy game developer in a fedora turned into a millionaire was an unexpected, very straight forward and compelling story from a gaming world where it was now notoriously difficult to identify the individual creators behind games.

But in 2011 it exploded. Minecraft became a phenomenon for real, was one of the fastest growing search terms on Google and had most videos associated with it on YouTube. The times when it was a sweet surprise for Markus to be recognized were forever gone.

IT'S RAINING AWARDS

Minecraft was also starting to get showered with awards. For his own part, the awards Markus won at the Independent Games Festival, the IGF, in San Francisco, were perhaps the finest of the lot. It is a bit like the indie world's Oscars and is held in the spring every year in connection with the biggest and most important game developer conference, GDC. At IGF, indie game developers from all over the world gather at their own party for an award ceremony where Swedes actually tend to win a lot of awards (one of the reasons for No More Sweden being arranged was that most Swedish indie developer did not have sufficient funds to travel to San Francisco, so they established their own festival).

Markus and Minecraft received, among other things, the Audience Award and the finest prize of them all, the Seumas McNally Grand Prize. While other indie developers certainly liked Markus and enjoyed him having his successes, there was also some muttering. Considering how little most indie developers actually earn, it simply felt wrong that Markus, who was already rich, would earn both more glory and prize checks. Even Anthony Carboni, the one who gave away the award, joked ironically about it onstage: "It truly warms my heart to see these guys win, they have had a really rough year. They need some cash," he said.

The award shower continued throughout 2011 and into 2012. The only other prize Markus accepted personally was a BAFTA in London in March 2012. BAFTA is Britain's counterpart to the Golden Globes or the Oscars, but since 1998 they also give out awards to video games. When Markus learned that he had received BAFTA's special prize, he tweeted that he was both "blown away" and "humbled." One of the reasons for awarding Markus with the prize was, according to BAFTA, that he was such a huge inspiration to all game developers.

For a while, Mojang received so many awards that someone came up with the idea that they would record a video at the office that could be sent as a thank you. Carl Manneh would walk up to Markus and say, "We won another award" and then Markus would become excited and say "great" and then give thanks, or something along those lines. Exactly what prize they had won would not be specified. In that way the same video could be used for all award ceremonies. "It would be a generic video," as Jens says in game development lingo.

But those exact words in that exact order is very difficult to say for a Swede. It is almost like one of these word games where you try to say something very fast, and it mostly comes out very wrong. Which Carl was about to discover. He went up to Markus and said: "We won ananan awand." Everyone laughed. It did not become a generic video, instead it became an inside joke that still is used whenever a new award is announced.

Mojang won ananan awand in Sweden too, at the annual Dataspelsgalan (which translates to something like the Video Game Gala). There they were, to everyone's surprise, awarded the Casual Game of the Year. Which was very strange, since if there is anything that Minecraft is not, it is casual. The definition of casual games is that they are supposed to be easy to understand, that you should be able to get started quickly and almost intuitively understand how to control the game.

With Minecraft, it is almost the exact opposite.

Not a very friendly game.

Honestly, in its basic design Minecraft is almost inhospitable to an inexperienced player. It is simply not playable unless you have some basic knowledge of gaming. Daniel Kaplan had both finished an education in game design at college level and worked as an indie developer for a few years before he came in contact with the game for the first time in 2009.

"When I started to play, I thought the design was crap. I didn't get it at all. I didn't know what to do or how to do it. I had to ask a few friends for help and they showed me. Then I discovered that it was a lot of fun, but if you look at how user friendly the game was, it was a disaster," he says.

Jens does not share Daniel's opinion though. When I asked him if he, like Daniel, or me for that matter, had any problems getting started with the game he looked at me in utter surprise and just said no. But then he has a different way of approaching video games in general; he is more fascinated by the rules behind a game than the game itself.

"I can buy a new board game, preferably a complicated strategy game, just to get to read the rules. I'm fascinated by the thoughts of those who made the game and what rules they created. If I'm at a party at someone else's house, sometimes I walk straight to the shelf with board games and pick out the rules for reading. I think it's very interesting," he says.

Well, most of us might not be as fascinated by the rules, as we are by the actual game that the rules are for. Fortunately, in a video game, most of the time you do not need to read the rules. Instead the player is often interactively led through the introduction. You are encouraged to, for example, move the left analog stick to look around in the game, and then to move the right stick to walk forward and back. Then the game asks you to run somewhere by pushing a special button, jump with another, pick up weapons with a third, shoot with a fourth and then reload with a fifth.

Although it can quickly become complicated if there are several buttons to keep track of, the game still often does a rather good job with these kinds of instructions. But not Minecraft.

The lack of instructions in the game that Markus made was at least partly unintentional. Those who first got to play Minecraft were people Markus knew from the forums he visited, hard core gamers and developers that just like Jens did not need instructions. In addition, Markus simply did not have time to make instructions in the beginning; it is not something a developer normally starts with anyway.

When it quickly turned out that the players were giving each other advice on how to play the game, there really was no point for Markus to give out any instructions. It suited him perfectly. Markus does not find instructions and tutorials any fun; instead he wants to encourage free thinking and experimenting. Soon, this became a part of Minecraft's appeal.

Without instructions, however, or knowing that one should look in forums and special Minecraft wikis online to receive tips and tricks, it was and still is hard for people who are not as used to games as Markus and Jens to play it. One who walked that road is Lydia Winters.

HEAD OF ALL THE FUN

Lydia has her workplace opposite Carl Manneh's. There she supports Minecraft's community, is in charge of media relations, deals with the fairs and events Mojang attends and various other projects. As soon as something involves standing on a stage to represent Mojang, Carl, Markus and Jakob assign her that role. It is a situation where none of them feels comfortable, but in which Lydia thrives. Then again, she is the director of fun.

Most of all she is managing the community, where all those millions of people who play Minecraft discuss it online, showcase their own builds and watch others'.

The Minecraft players are very active; about half of them log onto their game accounts every week, seven out of ten at least once a month. Those are high numbers compared to other games.

"My task is not so much to run the community as

Lydia Winters loves being in the spotlight, which is one of the reasons Markus, Jakob and Carl leave that to her as much as they can, as they did here at MineCon 2012 in Paris.

to supply it with material and just support everyone out there. The community really runs itself, it was there before I came aboard and it has a life of its own. To try to control it or govern it in any way wouldn't work. It would only be weird to even try," she says.

The fact is that the community is almost a force on its own. When a fan once asked Markus about how long he thinks Minecraft will survive and keep the community interested, he answered: "I think it's the other way round. As long as the community exists and YouTube works as it does, Minecraft will be there and function. It's not so much Minecraft that runs the community, but the community that runs Minecraft."

In 2010, Lydia Winters did not know any of this. Right about the same time that I was doing that first interview with Markus, she was sitting at home in St. Petersburg, Florida, thinking about what she should do next. She had worked as a kindergarten teacher and wedding photographer, and wanted to become famous and do something that aroused interest on the web. She had just finished a fundraiser for breast cancer research where she raised $20,000, including auctioning off private lessons with professional photographers. She had also shaved off her hair for donation to a charity that made wigs for cancer patients.

"I had just started my own YouTube channel where I talked about different things. But soon I had difficulties coming up with new ideas for subjects to talk about. I wanted to make one episode every day, but it was harder than I expected. It wasn't exactly a success; I was pleased if I had 30 views on one of the videos," she says.

In November she started to panic. She felt that she needed something solid to hold on to, one subject to build her own channel around. But she did not have any good ideas. So she called her friend Vu Bui in Los Angeles.

When this was written in January 2013, Vu was Mojang's latest permanent employee, but he had worked for them as a subcontractor since fall 2011. At Mojang they have a saying that goes "no matter what job you have had,

Vu has had it too." Which actually seems to be worryingly correct — the man is after all just 35 years old. By that time though, he was neither a realtor nor a public speaker, but ran an online photo business with his brother that focused on taking pictures of and filming online celebrities. (It is still online at Thebuibrothers.com.) He and Lydia had met several years before through their photography. When Lydia called, Vu and his brother had just met one of internet's more famous trend spotters.

"We had actually asked him about what was the hottest online trend right now. Or the question was rather what one should invest in right now if one wanted to build a successful channel on YouTube. He told us that Minecraft was really hot, and that it was probably what you should do. But neither my brother nor I was interested at the time. We hadn't even heard of Minecraft," says Vu.

THE MISADVENTURES OF MINECRAFTCHICK

So when Lydia called and asked, Vu simply related what the trend spotter had said: Go for Minecraft.

"I didn't have any better ideas so why not? I had never played Minecraft, actually I had never even played any video game whatsoever. But Vu thought that was good. Use it as your own thing, he said. Make videos about how someone who has never played before makes her way through Minecraft."

On November 15, 2010, Lydia posted her first video, barely four minutes long. In the autumn of 2012, two years later, it had been viewed by almost 200,000 people, but when it was first published it passed almost unnoticed. Only Vu and a few other friends watched it. Because Lydia had shaved her hair off, she was wearing a pink wig. She did not have any good names for her show either, so while waiting for something better she chose MinecraftChick.

"I had a bad name and a bad show. It wasn't good. You can see me in the lower corner of the shot and what I was playing in the middle. I didn't even know how to make Minecraft cover the entire screen, it was just a small square in the middle, and then the rest was gray and ugly. And I didn't know how to play. I mean, I didn't know at all," she says.

"At first I couldn't move, I didn't know that you had to press *W*, *A*, *S*, and *D* to walk in different directions. And once I got it I fell down in the water and drowned. I just couldn't get up. I didn't know that you should press the space bar to jump out of the water. It felt as if I was making the world's worst video."

But if you look at the video today, you can see that Lydia made a production that was much better than a lot of other things on YouTube, especially at that time. She altered the game clips with short clips of herself and therefore created 3:44 minutes with a surprisingly high entertainment value, especially for being the first episode. Even if it was a bit chaotic and unorganized, it was clear that she had both ambition and an idea about how she wanted to make her videos.

She made one episode per day for 10 days. By the second episode she had already realized that you are supposed to look at walkthroughs on YouTube, forums and wikis to learn how to play. Without knowing it, she was documenting — in a slightly twisted manner — the same journey that millions of players had already made, were making at the same time as her and are making right now in Minecraft. Every day her number of views increased, reaching several hundreds. Lydia felt like an internet phenomena. Someone had also commented and said that the videos were like the misadventures of MinecraftChick. That is how Lydia's show got its final name.

"I thought it sounded both right and fun, because I was really having misadventures. No matter what I did, it turned out wrong. When a creeper blew me up for the first time, I didn't understand what was happening. I got really scared."

But by Thanksgiving 2010 something troubling happened. Less than two weeks after the premiere, everything seemed to go wrong.

"When I woke up and checked my account it said that I had over 2,000 subscribers. It was 10 times more than what I had when I went to bed the night before. And I had received hundreds of emails. I got angry and upset. Just when I thought everything was finally taking off, someone had hacked my account. I was upset and really angry," she remembers.

What had really happened though was that Lydia had had her first encounter with the Minecraft fans online. When she read some of the emails, which turned out to be personal and not spam, she realized that some of the bigger Minecraft channels on YouTube had mentioned her show, which instantly led to the dramatic increase in subscribers. On the internet, as you know, everything is only a few clicks away.

When Lydia finally met Markus, Carl and the others for the first time in the summer of 2011, she had about 200,000 subscribers and was, by her own words, six months away from being able to live off AdWords, the advertising revenue generated from Google-owned YouTube.

"I quickly went from not knowing anything about Minecraft, to being fascinated by both it and the community. Then I discovered that it was Mojang that made the game and that they were located in Stockholm; I became interested in them also. I mean, the game and the whole thing was amazing, so I thought Markus and the others at Mojang were amazing too."

A love and fascination that were to be returned.

4
A GAME
NEVER READY

"A game has to be finished at some point, and that felt like as good a time as ever," says Markus.

He is referring to Mojang's first game conference of their own, MineCon, held in November 2011 in Las Vegas. The choice of name is obvious for anyone who likes video games. Blizzard, the developers of World of Warcraft, have their BlizzCon; the Doom creators Id Software have their QuakeCon (they made Quake after Doom); and whoever watches the TV show *The Big Bang Theory* knows that nerds who like superheroes go on a pilgrimage to Comic-Con. So when Mojang arranged their own con, 5,000 fans from 24 countries came to Las Vegas to meet their idols and Minecraft friends.

"It was both amazing and a bit crazy. It was our first

conference, and to take care of 5,000 visitors, even if they do love you, is not an easy undertaking. There were a lot of things that didn't work out the way we had planned, but at the end it still turned out as a great event. Personally, I enjoy those situations, where everything happens at once and no one has any real control," says Vu Bui who, together with Lydia Winters, handled most of the practical things regarding the conference.

Lydia was hired by Mojang after having volunteered for them during the big gaming convention E3 in Los Angeles earlier that summer. She did such a good job that she was permanently hired on the spot. Moving to Stockholm was not a problem for her, but first she had to stay in Florida to take care of MineCon. This turned out to be too big of a project for her. So she asked Carl if she could hire her friend Vu, the man who has had every job there is. Carl said yes, and thereby probably saved the whole convention.

This does not prevent Daniel Kaplan from sighing deeply when I ask, slightly carelessly, just over a month after the event, if there will be another MineCon in 2012.

"Maybe, or no, I doubt it. I almost hope not. It was so much work involved that I don't know if we have the time or energy. We're only a small game studio, not a big event company. It took a lot of energy," he says.

Even Jens remembers the whole thing with certain trepidation. Like when they organized a charity dinner. People bought expensive tickets so that they could have dinner with the Mojangstas. Jens arrived tired and hungry, with the naive hope of enjoying a quiet dinner together with the fans.

"But I barely had time to eat, I just about managed to shove in some of it. It was a pity, the food was very nice. There were so many people who wanted to talk, take pictures and get autographs. I can understand that, they had paid for it. But it was at the edge of what I could handle. Afterwards I had to go to my room and just lie down for a bit."

One who enjoyed it more was, a bit surprisingly, Markus himself. "I think we should have a MineCon every year as long as Minecraft is this big," he says.

"I think it's good; it ties us and the community closer together in a very obvious way. Otherwise it can get so separated, that we at Mojang are one thing and those who play another."

A DRUNKEN FACILITATOR

What Markus has made a habit of doing at special occasions, like MineCon, is to arrange a huge private party where he invites all visitors 18 and over as well as other indie game developers and friends. Markus has a thing for electro-house DJs (like Swedish House Mafia) and always hires one of the world's top names. This time it was Canadian Deadmau5 (pronounced "dead mouse"). I have noticed that Markus shares his taste in music with many other game makers of his age in Sweden. I wondered if it was because, as the name electro-house indicates, a lot of the music is done with and on computers. Markus has, of course, an altogether different explanation:

"In my case it's about a subculture. Electronic techno music was big amongst the developers I found myself with at the time. It quickly became an identity thing, that later developed into a social thing between us. There are groups of game developers in the U.S. where hard rock is the big thing, a music style that's not connected to computers or anything. So it's definitely more coincidence, where you happen to be at a certain time."

When Markus went to one of Swedish House Mafia's farewell concerts in November 2012 in Stockholm he tweeted: "Swedish House Mafia just exploded my head." After that short sentence he wrote a heart. That is a love that sometimes is answered. Whoever follows Markus on Twitter has noticed that he and Deadmau5 are friends and that they sometimes have intense dialogues. And as everyone knows, even if electro-house once was a subculture, it is very much mainstream now.

Alex Chapman, the London-based lawyer who represents Mojang, has worked with all kinds of artists, even though he has become more specialized at indie game developers in recent years. He also sees a different effect of Markus's close association with Deadmau5 and other artists.

"Markus is the first modern rock star in the gaming world. The fact that he's friends with Deadmau5 on Twitter enhances that image. The kids read his and Deadmau5's dialogue and to them there is no difference between a superstar who does music and another who makes video games."

In Las Vegas, Deadmau5 did not make Lydia's and Vu's heads explode. He did however play while something happened in their hearts. With a little bit of help from the CEO. Carl Manneh explains: "When MineCon finished, it was like being able to breathe for the first time in a month for me. It had been so much work and tension getting that whole thing off. Of course I drank a little too much at Markus's party. And of course I had one of those smart ideas you tend to get when you have one drink too many. I'd seen that Lydia and Vu liked each other so I walked up to them and said something along the lines of 'you guys are made for each other, you really should be together.' You know, those ideas you regret the next day."

He did not regret that one though. What he said actually did the trick.

"Well, Carl can't take credit for us becoming a couple, but he facilitated it. After he said that at the Deadmau5 party, the next step was easy. We had our first date the next day," Vu says.

ALPHA AND BETA

Even though the official release of Minecraft was a big deal at MineCon in Las Vegas, to say it was actually finished is somewhat of an overstatement. That is why Jens is still working on the game.

When Markus first launched the game online in June 2009, it was in its so-called alpha stage — a very early, but playable version of a game. If you choose to play the free version of Minecraft today on the computer, you have to settle with the alpha version, though it is from early 2010 instead of 2009.

From alpha, a game goes to a beta stage before eventually being finished (if you know Greek, you know that alpha means *A*, and beta *B*). Most game productions are not shown to outsiders, neither in its alpha nor its beta stage, but only when it is completely finished. If you ever get to see a game before it is completed, you have to sign a document where you promise not to reveal anything and that you understand that it is an unfinished production you have seen. It is all very hush-hush. I have lost count of all so-called NDAs (non-disclosure agreements) I have signed. At many studios, NDAs are lying in the reception ready to be signed; you sign them at the same time as you write your name on the visitor list. It is a standard procedure. This is the only way you, as an outsider, can even enter the premises; it does not matter if you are a journalist or a craftsman. As I said, I have signed many. And broken a few.

Markus did it the other way round: he launched an early, very much unfinished, edition of Minecraft online.

"It took some guts. It's a scary thing to do, show a game that you're not finished with. But it's a lot better than not showing it. Besides, that scary feeling only holds on a short while," says Markus.

By letting people play the game so early, Markus got their response on what they thought was fun and what they wanted more of in the game. He updated it constantly, almost daily.

"I was very open with everything from the start. I wrote on forums and on my blog. I think that's what made people dare to buy Minecraft, even though it wasn't finished. I guess they enjoyed the game and thought it was fun, but they also trusted that I would eventually finish it," he says.

Once you had paid for the game, you never had to pay again. That was also an innovative approach. Normally, instead of improving an old game for free you make a new one and sell it. If Markus had followed the norm, he would have frozen Minecraft in November 2011. Everything that Jens had done since then would then be kept secret so that it could later be launched as a sequel, Minecraft 2. It is not so much greed as normal business; to develop games takes time and costs a lot of money, so of course you have to charge for it. But Markus did not do that — it is the constant in-flow of new players that earns Mojang money, not selling sequels.

Markus also discovered that there was a financial aspect to constantly updating the game; it made people talk about it online and that attracted new customers. That was not the original reason he did it, but it was certainly a nice consequence. To release a highly unfinished game and then continue developing it for everyone to see while people continued playing it was, surprisingly enough, a genius business move. Although, he had no such ulterior motives.

"No, there is no strategy behind anything that has happened. It feels as if it just turned out this way. I haven't done any of this on purpose," he says.

A CINDERELLA STORY

When you read about someone who has already made it in life, it often seems like everything that has happened in that person's life has led inevitably to their success. Even obvious coincidences and setbacks in that person's youth seem, in retrospect, to fit the picture.

Looking at Markus's life now, you can see that all his life has pointed to this moment. But if you would have met him in his childhood or youth, chances are that you would have wondered what would become of the boy.

Because the truth about Markus is that throughout his childhood, he was one of the kids who never really fit in, who did not like sports, really sucked at soccer and would rather sit at home building Lego, sit by the computer or, possibly, be a game master when he played pen-and-paper role-playing games with his friends. Today we talk about

Just a few years back, no one knew who Markus "Notch" Persson was. Now he is among the gaming world's richest and most famous. Still he is not very comfortable with being interviewed or having his photo taken: "I am still a shy guy."

the revenge of the nerds, and one of the world's most popular TV shows is one about a group of nerds. During the '80s and '90s? Not so much revenge for that specific group. It was rather the opposite. As if being classified a nerd was not uncool enough, Markus's family were also Pentecostals, something that was, and still is, not exactly mainstream in Sweden.

Markus grew up in Salem, just south of Stockholm, with his parents Birger and Ritva and his younger sister Anna. Throughout Markus's childhood, the family situation seems to have been safe and stable, but when his father left the family and fell back into drug abuse when Markus was in his early teens, the situation became a lot messier.

Birger did, however, enjoy both computers and games and bought Markus a Commodore 128 when he was in first grade. It is almost like his entire life got its direction that day. He immediately started playing the simple games that existed at the time, and also to make his own according to the instructions that came with the games (games that he had to trash every night, since there was no way to save them on Commodore 128). It appears as if a big part of Markus's childhood and youth was spent there, in front of a computer. School was so easy for him that he started staying home more. In high school he was so superior in programming that he did not even have to attend classes. Markus was simply too smart for school, so smart he sometimes had a hard time being motivated to study and excel. Which, by the way, seems to be a thing he has in common with many of the other developers at Mojang.

College was never even talked of. It did not seem to be necessary either, because Markus graduated in the middle of the late '90s internet boom and quickly landed a job at a web agency. They welcomed anyone as skilled at coding as Markus with open arms.

"Back then there was no college level education on the making of video games. Back then you had to train at home and learn it by yourself. Today there are actually a lot of good educations out there. But if someone asks me how to become a game developer, I usually reply that you should just start making games on your own. What programming language or tool you use is not that important, the important thing is that you start making games. I even try to avoid telling what my favorite tools or languages are. Otherwise there's a big risk that people think that that's the key to success. It's not. The key is to try yourself and discover how much fun you can have."

In the middle of the '00s he got his first game developing job, for the website King.com. The company focused on making casual games, often based on famous game concepts like board games or a few well-established computer game genres. It might not have been Markus's cup of tea, but the years there taught him at least one important lesson.

"I learnt how to finish games. If there's anything you need to learn as an indie developer, it's that. I've made countless of half-finished games throughout the years," he says.

JENS IS PRETTY WRONG

It is fair to say that Minecraft is under constant development. Not big revolutions or new directions for the game, but continual small steps. Jens releases news every other week. The weeks when he is not publishing news, he often shows future updates in so-called snapshots. The players can choose themselves if they want to check it out more carefully by pressing a link, or wait until Jens thinks that

Not only do young Minecrafters like to dress up as characters from their beloved game, they are also an active bunch. Half of the 20 million people who have bought the game log into their account at least once a week.

the new features are good enough to be added to the game. Then it shows up automatically. Every new major feature is immediately turned into walkthroughs by fans on YouTube.

"Sometimes I get a bit tired of constantly making new things. Of course, the fans are expecting it, we have actually set the speed ourselves. Although, sometimes I think, but please, can you not just play what is already out there, there are so many things to do in the game already," he says.

That is about as close to complaining as he gets. I have never met a man as patient as Jens. Patient and sweet. For example, when he writes an autograph he does not want to write it too fast. He wants to look everyone in their eyes. And so he does, politely and gently, no matter how many people there are. I have seen it with my own eyes; I even have it on camera.

He also says things that I find very nice. He told me once that he rarely works overtime because he and his girlfriend Jenny Thornell, or 242_girl as she calls herself on Twitter, take turns cooking dinner. So when I saw him and Jenny at a Mojang party, I asked Jenny if Jens was a good cook. She said yes, he is really good. Jens did not agree: "No, I can't say that I'm good at it, but there's one thing I'm good at. If I make a mistake, I learn from it and won't repeat it again." Jenny just said oh, hugged his arm and smiled with her entire face.

At the same party, around half past 10, when I was about to leave, I ran into Jens again. I said hi and wondered if he was leaving too. His response: "No, I'm going home at 11." It may sound a bit square in writing, but really not when Jens says it.

Jens's sweetness really showed itself one late night in Paris. Markus had had his big MineCon 2012 closing party (yes, they had a MineCon in 2012 too, more about that later) at Luc Besson's movie studio in Paris, right by the huge, national soccer stadium, Stade de France. It was half past three in the morning, and even though there had been a big party there were very few taxis. The ones that arrived were all pre-booked and the drivers refused, in a very non-French way, to drive anyone other than the person who had ordered their car — whether any such person actually was there or not, no matter how long the car had to wait it seemed.

In the middle of all this Jens, 242_girl, their friends from Oxeye and Daniel's parents, who naturally are a bit older, came along. In some way the group managed to get a large cab. Jens, however, refused to get in before the elderly couple had also squeezed in, so he stood outside the car the longest. "Come now," said Jenny who wanted him to get in before Daniel's parents so he could sit next to her. "Please get in," said the driver who thought they were taking too long a time. "No," said Jens, "the most important is that they get a ride home." In the end, he also fit in the minivan after a lot of switching places and squeezing together. I assume that it is almost the same side of Jens that showed when I once asked if he is a good programmer.

"No, I wouldn't say that. I think my strengths are that I'm pretty good at a lot of things. I'm pretty good at programming, pretty good at graphics and pretty good at handling social medias," he says.

And I thought that he might be pretty wrong in that self-assessment.

MINECRAFT ONLINE

Some of the things Jens does with the game are simpler, and others considerably harder. The more difficult things can, for example, be making it easier for players to start their own servers so that they can play with each other online. The idea was for Minecraft to be like other games in that aspect: just a button to press and you will be connected to a server and can play online. Originally it was called Minecraft Online, later changed to Minecraft Realms. It was supposed to happen during 2012, but it turns out that Jens and the others were being too optimistic. Not only was this due to technical difficulties, it was also because Carl Manneh and Alex Chapman wanted to negotiate the best deal possible with those who are to deliver the actual server solution.

The biggest reason why the online problem was so technically difficult to solve was Markus himself. He admitted it bluntly.

"It was a mistake that taught me many things. The tricky thing when you make a game by yourself is not to paint yourself into a corner. It is really the only thing you can do that's really wrong. Maybe you don't have to solve all the problems or add all the features you want in the game from the beginning, however you have to try to create windows that make it easier to add things later on," he says.

And this is what he missed when he built Minecraft — to create that window that would make it easy to add a service like Minecraft Realms.

The online service will generate a lot of money for

Mojang. "When we get it all in place it can very well be Mojang's biggest source of income so far," says Carl.

Considering how much money Minecraft already pulls in, Carl's words almost make you dizzy. But since you only pay for the game once and then play for free forever, even though they update the game constantly, there is of course a risk that the flow of incoming gamers — and thus income — will eventually decline. If you want to use Realms, you would have to subscribe to it instead. But Mojang could not get there until late 2013, even though Carl spent many late nights in phone conferences with companies on the U.S. West Coast. (It is a nine-hour time difference, so when people start working at 9 a.m. in Seattle or San Francisco, the time is then 6 p.m. in Sweden.)

A NICE THING TO FIX

Another big problem concerns all the things players create themselves for the game, so-called mods. Mod is short for modification and is an addition or some form of expansion of a game that the players create on their own. It is common in the gaming world, especially when it comes to computer games. Entire games have been made as mods, like Counter-Strike and Team Fortress. Many successful game developers have actually started their careers by making mods.

In the Minecraft world there is, of course, an extreme

amount of add-ons and mods, which is what happens when you have so many dedicated players as Minecraft has (and do not be surprised if many future game developers will consider Minecraft the starting point of their career). The problem though, is that Markus did not make an easy system or interface (although Jens does not call it interface, instead he calls it API, which is short for application programming interface) for these mods and expansions to be added and then stay in the game. What happens now — and what has always happened — is that all different kinds of mods crash as soon as Jens updates the game. Which, of course, he does all the time. The person who made the mod then has to fix it by hand so that it starts working again.

As Jens says, "It would be nice to at least fix it so that the players' things don't break all the time."

The most popular thing Jens can do, though, is to add new things such as blocks or animals. It is also simpler than the bigger changes. Although, it is also starting to get more difficult. The game is simply getting so full of things that you cannot fit more in it.

"So far we've solved it by removing things. If I add something new to a world, I also have to remove something else. The texture is just too small. That's also something we have to redo. It's not that complicated, I know how to solve it, I just haven't had time."

That the texture is too small is similar to having too small a canvas when you paint.

And even if things will fit, it can still be difficult.

"I'm going to make birds that can hang upside down in the ceilings of the caves," Jens told me in the summer of 2012.

"But nothing in the game is made to be upside down. Markus didn't think about that when he built it, that's why it's a bit complicated to make such a seemingly easy thing. For example, I have to convert so that the birds' visual field is calculated from the feet. It's really not that hard."

After saying that Jens was sitting quiet for a few moments, thinking about what he just said. Then he added, "But it's not that easy either."

5
NO COFFEE, THANKS

Four people are sitting in the smallest room at Åsögatan. It is the entire Scrolls team, with Jakob Porser at the front. When I enter the room in February 2012, the spirit is high. Which is a bit surprising actually.

In September 2011, a lawsuit against Mojang was submitted to the Stockholm District Court. The media giant ZeniMax thought that Jakob and his team were guilty of trademark infringement.

Being sued by an American media company for such things can scare even the most seasoned. The outcomes of legal disputes like that are hard to predict, especially in the U.S. with its complicated and often-critiqued laws surrounding copyright and trademarks. To take up the fight in such a battle as a small indie developer would be foolish,

big success on Facebook with its game Candy Crush Saga. In 2013, that game took off on mobiles, and within a few months it became the world's most played game with some 100 million daily active users. It also brought King from obscurity in the gaming industry to prominence. But back in Jakob and Markus's days, the studio was hardly even viewed as a "real" developer by its peers in Stockholm and Sweden. Candy Crush Saga gives you an idea of what kind of games they were doing: not as polished or as big as that, but games that were colorful, easy to learn but hard to master and always built around core game mechanics. Other new popular King games are Pet Rescue Saga, Bubble Witch Saga and Farm Heroes Saga.

It was not the most prestigious workplace for game developers back in 2006. But Markus and Jakob liked it there, not least because they had such a good relationship with their coworkers. The tempo was high; they finished a game roughly every other month. The target group was, according to Jakob, middle-aged women (King.com themselves states that 75 percent of their players today are women between the ages of 25 and 50, so I guess exactly what counts as middle age is in the eye of the beholder). When they were not working, they were fantasizing about a different kind of game.

Just like Markus, Jakob had been playing video games his entire life. He had even made a few of his own that were lying around at home in some drawer. He had never visited any forum for game developers, though, and he was not particularly comfortable with the term indie.

No, Murloc from World of Warcraft did not come to life: this is Jakob Porser taking a break by playing pinball. But no one in the office stands a chance against Jens and Aron, the resident champions.

"I've not been like Markus at all in that way. I still don't feel quite comfortable with the term indie, I don't really know what it stands for," he says.

This did not stop a deep and creative friendship from forming. Jakob also noticed how talented Markus was.

"He often came with very good solutions and ideas for problems you had. He has a very good sense of what can be fun in a game. It comes naturally to him, I think it's a gut feeling."

In hindsight, it can be a bit hard to understand why Markus, or Jakob for that matter, did not go straight to the successful Swedish game industry, to the companies and studios that made Sweden famous as one of the world's most important and most successful countries in the field. The truth is simply that the Swedish gaming industry had not quite taken off back then. The time between 2004, when Markus started at King.com, and 2010, when Jacob quit, was exactly the time when Swedish game development stepped forward for real, and what is called the Swedish gaming miracle arose.

Dice took the lead with their Battlefield 1942, a game that can be viewed as the starting point of what later happened. During these years, Dice made several sequels and new versions of Battlefield, they created the groundbreaking Mirror's Edge and made a couple of games in the new series Battlefield: Bad Company. In 2006, the studio was bought by Electronic Arts, the world's biggest game publisher.

Avalanche released Just Cause 1 and 2. Starbreeze came with their breakthrough game The Chronicles of Riddick. In the meantime, the game studio Grin basically came out of nowhere, grew to having 300 employees and then went bankrupt, all in a few years. In Malmö, Massive Entertainment made World in Conflict, got sold to Vivendi and then to Ubisoft. The growth between 2004 and 2010 was simply huge. To say that the landscape of the Swedish gaming industry changed during this period is a staggering understatement.

However, Markus did actually make an attempt to get

into the "real" game industry. He applied and got a job at Avalanche Studios, but did not at all like being a small cog in a big machine. He quit and returned to King.com and Jakob after just a week or two. Avalanche's founder and manager, Christofer Sundberg, did not even have time to notice that Markus worked there; he read about it afterwards.

OUR VERY OWN ROLE-PLAYING GAME

During the years at King, Markus and Jakob had time to bounce many ideas off each other. One of them was about making a digital version of the role-playing games played as collectible card games. The most popular of them was, and still is, Magic: The Gathering. The game saw daylight in 1993 and today there are several editions of it, including a computer version. According to Wikipedia there are roughly 12 million people playing Magic, but only a fraction of them online. There are many more role-playing card games than that, but they all work on almost the same principles.

"Both Markus and I had played these kind of games a lot when we were younger, and we also played it with each other during our time at King. We had a bunch of ideas on how to turn it into a computer game."

Collectible card games are a bit like bridge or poker, just a lot more imaginative and complex. Plus it involves a lot more feelings for your cards than ordinary card games. It can go like this: each player plays as a wizard and has cards with different values and abilities. One card might show a monster, for example a goblin. To play a card you need energy, and you can get energy in different ways. In Pokémon, which also is a collectible card game, you can get energy by pulling an energy card from your deck. A hand needs a good mix of energy and Pokémon cards; energy is needed to play out cards, but without Pokémons you have no cards to play out.

In this example, our goblin has a certain attack value, one in defense, and also a number for how many rounds the card has to rest before being used again. Other cards can give the monster extra abilities and spells, or they can cast magic against the opponents cards. If you play out a goblin that has three attack points against a priest with five in defense, three lives are subtracted from his five. If someone later attacks the priest with two or more points in attack, the priest dies. Unless the person who has the priest plays out a card which gives the priest extra life. And so on.

There is almost no limit to how complex a game can be, because in addition you can decide what kind of deck you are going to use from the beginning, and hence decide what basic strategy to play with, for example defense, attack or magic. A lot of effort goes into gathering cards and getting a good deck. The more cards you have, the more freedom you have to make a deck that suits you. That is why you talk about collectible card games.

"We felt that it would be a thrill making our own version of a game like that, but as a computer game. There really weren't any good games out there. And above all, we felt that this was a game that we would want to play ourselves. That's what's most important," says Jakob.

EVERYONE NEEDS SHOELACES

In 2009, Markus switched jobs, from being a game developer at King to being a regular programmer at Jalbum, an online photo service while Jakob remained at King.com.

It was at Jalbum that Markus met Carl Manneh for the first time. About the same time as Markus began his career at King.com, Carl had launched his own first online business. His wife was working as a model in Vancouver, and not liking to be idle Carl came up with a business idea for an online store.

"It wasn't exactly a master plan. I was sitting at Starbucks, trying to come up with ideas. I looked down at people's feet and saw all the shoelaces and thought aha, everyone needs shoelaces." So he opened a store for funny shoelaces, Sneakerlaces.com.

"It was an okay business, not a smash hit or anything. Most importantly, I learned a lot starting that business. When we moved back from Vancouver in 2005, I was able to sell the company."

Back in Sweden Carl landed a job as the head of a small online newcomer, the photo service Jalbum. And that was where his and Markus's paths first crossed.

"We had a problem that needed solving and someone who knew Markus from a forum was aware that he had worked with that type of programming before. We contacted him and eventually we met at our office. He didn't like the idea of working as a consultant. It didn't seem like he wanted to deal with billing and those kinds of things. This was right before the weekend. He didn't promise to fix anything for us, he just said we'll see, that maybe he'd get around to it."

However, on Monday morning, an email was waiting from Markus with a finished solution. All you had to do was to install it and go, problem solved. "Pay whatever you think it is worth" was the closest to a bill Carl got.

"It was such a nice way, just solving the problem first before discussing money and other things. We decided to try to hire him."

Which was not an easy thing. It took almost a year to lure Markus from King to Jalbum, and the main reason he eventually accepted was that he wanted to work more on Minecraft. That was why a programming job was preferable to game developing at King, who also had rules against employees making games outside work — especially if you charged for the game.

It did not work for Markus, who had high hopes of making an okay salary from Minecraft.

"Markus told us about the game from the get-go and I didn't see a problem with it. I didn't understand much of it, saw it more as a nice hobby project. But after only two months he made more money from Minecraft than he did working at Jalbum," remembers Carl.

Markus did not want to quit because of this, though; instead he chose, with Carl's blessing, to cut down on his work hours.

CARL KNOWS WHO TO HIRE

After a year at Jalbum, Markus finally did quit to spend all of his time on Minecraft. It was also then that his and Jakob's dreams about starting their own game studio began taking shape for real.

As Jakob says: "The thoughts about starting a studio had been there a while, but maybe more as a dream than anything that would actually happen. They became more serious in the spring of 2010. Minecraft was doing so well then that there was enough money to start something together. But it wasn't just because there was money. Markus's successes gave both me and other developers inspiration. It gave us a hope and a belief in that it was possible to make games after your own head and still make money off it."

Therefore, it was also time to develop new ideas for games. But even though they tested quite a few new game concepts in Markus's kitchen, they kept coming back to that collectible card game. It soon became clear that that was what they would start off with when they formed their own studio, which would be named Mojang. Or rather, Markus would continue with Minecraft and Jacob would devote his time to Scrolls, which is the name they chose for the new game.

However, one obstacle remained. It was the summer when Valve's developers blogged about Markus. It certainly increased the sales of Minecraft, but the fact that they offered him a first class trip to their office in Seattle also meant there was a big risk that Markus would get an offer he could not refuse from every game developer's dream employer.

"Of course Markus had to go, you can't get any more cred than working for Valve. Maybe I wasn't too worried that he would accept a position there, but at the same time I didn't know what they would offer him. Maybe they wanted to buy Minecraft. Anything could happen, as far as I knew."

But when Markus called after his meeting with Valve he had a pretty straightforward message for his friend back in Sweden: You can quit your job, he said to Jakob, who did just that the very next day.

"Both Markus and I knew that we needed someone to deal with the business side of things. Markus was sick of dealing with such things. He had taken care of the customer support, the economy, and everything else with Minecraft for a year all by himself. He didn't need that in his life anymore. And I wasn't up to it either. So we thought that we better find someone who could take care of those things. We didn't think it was less important than making games, we just didn't want to do it ourselves."

Carl Manneh is not your ordinary CEO. As CEO of Mojang, he's something of a star to the millions of Minecraft fans. "Signing autographs felt weird in the beginning; now it's just fun."

That is why they turned to Carl to get tips on a suitable CEO. It turned out that he knew exactly whom they should turn to.

"It wasn't hard to see the possibilities with Mojang, there was already a successful product, a strong cash flow and good liquidity. I also knew that I worked well with Markus. It was an easy choice to tip them about me," Carl says and smiles.

The company was formed in October 2010, but because it took some time for Carl and Jakob to leave their current jobs, Daniel Kaplan and Jens Bergensten were both at the office before them. The graphic designer Junkboy (Markus Toivonen is his real name) was also hired.

Jens was initially hired to work on Scrolls, but how do you work on a game that only exists in someone's head — especially when that person is not even there? There was not much else for him to do but to start helping Markus out with Minecraft.

"I wasn't even supposed to work with it, but since I was here and it seemed like Markus could use a helping hand I gave him one. Then we just kept going. Our way of thinking about games is very similar. We have the same view about a lot of things, that made it very easy."

THE GAME THAT IS NEVER FINISHED

Scrolls is starting to take on almost mythological status in the Mojang and Minecraft world. It is the game that is never really finished. When I met Jakob in May 2012, his plan was for it to be ready for sales in early September. Scrolls would not follow Minecraft's path completely though. An alpha version of the game would not be made available for sales.

"Minecraft is the perfect game to be released the way Markus did. You can build layers upon layers of content as time goes. Scrolls doesn't work like that. There has to be a lot more finished content and more functions in place before it's fun to play for a longer period of time," Jakob explains.

That is why the plan was to not launch Scrolls until

it reached the beta stage. According to the plan, it should then be an additional six months until Scrolls should be polished enough to be officially released and thus sold for full price. The plan did not work out however. When the year came to its end, they still had not launched Scrolls. It was not until the summer of 2013 that the game was polished enough to be released in beta.

"There's more work than we first thought. There are a few technical challenges, like creating good matchmaking when playing online and having a system that prevents cheating. Also all cards have to be drawn and also have their own animations, which takes time. The cards can't be released half-done, they all have to be finished. There also has to be enough cards to create a good depth in the gaming experience."

It is partly these cards that are the reason why there are so many people working on the game. They simply need many graphic artists. Jakob designs and programs the actual game. Three graphic artists work full-time with it and Junkboy helps as much as time allows him. Additionally, Daniel Frisk has worked with the servers and online functions, which really was Jens's job. Frisk used to be an IT architect at Jalbum, but he eventually followed Carl to Mojang. He was the one who had known about Markus's skills from online forums.

Many doubted Scrolls' chances of success. "When large companies like Warner and others have visited us they just shake their heads. You already have Minecraft, why not make Minecraft 2 instead of a small niche game, they wonder. From a pure business standpoint it's hard to argue with that," says Jakob.

"But we're not telling ourselves that there is the same market for Scrolls as there is for a sandbox game like Minecraft. We think perhaps of hundreds of thousands of players rather than millions. If we would always aim at making games as big as Minecraft, we would constantly be disappointed," says Jakob.

"One of the basic ideas when starting Mojang was to always make the games we wanted to, the games we wanted to play ourselves. We wanted to be a company that didn't look at the market research or adapted the game idea to something other than what we thought was fun ourselves. We've had the economy to have that approach from the start, and I honestly think it's just as good as any.

"You can never really know for sure if people are going to like what you make anyhow. The only thing you can do is your very best and then hope that others will enjoy it as much as you do. If Scrolls would fail, I can at least be proud. Then I'd have a breakdown, pick myself up and start all over with a new game idea."

CAN YOU OWN A WORD?

But then there was ZeniMax, with two of the world's most reputable game studios under their wings. One of them is id Software, the company that once made both Doom and Quake, which are two of the games that have influenced Markus the most. The other is Bethesda Softworks, which has made a name for itself with its role-playing game series The Elder Scrolls, which Markus has also devoted a lot of time to.

And that was where the problem lay. In the word "scrolls." In Mojang's game, the collector cards have the form of old scrolls, hence the name Scrolls.

What appears to have set the whole thing in motion was Mojang wanting to protect the trademark Minecraft in 2011. It went without problems, but to save time and money they also included the name Scrolls in the process. Thus alarming the media giant. Jakob was on vacation when the conflict started and he was therefore the last person in the office to hear about it.

"It was a really weird feeling finding out. I was not prepared at all. We had many discussions about what we were going to do. It was not that the name Scrolls was all that vital to us; after all it was just a name of a very unfinished game. But we thought that what was happening was wrong. Both the name thing and a big game company bullying a small one. So we decided to fight back. The worst that could happen was that we would lose and have to rename the game, but in that case it would've at least given Scrolls some attention."

To Markus, there was never any other option.

"It may have been wrong of us to try to protect the trademark Scrolls to begin with, but it felt wrong that someone could own a generic word that's just part of a longer title. Besides, scrolls is a word that's often used in the role-playing context, it's not like Bethesda invented it."

But ZeniMax refused to listen to that reasoning. When Carl wrote an email to one of the big shots in the company and offered to fly to them and talk about it over a cup of coffee, he got the uninviting answer: I don't drink coffee.

ZeniMax filed the lawsuit to the Stockholm District Court in September 2011. A month later the court ruled in Mojang's favor.

It was mainly Alex Chapman, with intellectual rights to games as his primary work area, who handled the legalities. He spent a lot of time in the beginning of 2012 negotiating with ZeniMax, who not only were starting to realize that they had a weak case but also a rich and determined opponent in Mojang. They also received a lot of online criticism from gamers, not only Minecraft fans. The discussion was so hotheaded that Bethesda felt compelled to point out that it actually was not them, but the lawyers at the parent company that quarreled. In March, Chapman finally settled with ZeniMax. Mojang got a license to make Scrolls but had to promise never to make a sequel with the same name.

"It was one of my finest moments as a lawyer," says Chapman. "ZeniMax got what they wanted, and Mojang didn't have to give anything up. Mojang's way of doing games is to never make sequels. There are none and there has never been any plan on making a sequel to Scrolls. Instead the game will be updated and improved infinitely as long as people are playing it; that's the way Mojang does their games. That settlement was a real beauty."

IT IS A BIT DUMBED DOWN

Early during the summer of 2012, Mojang released a closed alpha version of Scrolls. It meant that only those who were invited could play the game. My son and I were invited, but we found it hard to get caught up in it. There was not enough content to make it fun for more than a few hours and it was also hard to find anyone to play against online. Only about a hundred people had been let into the game and that was simply not enough.

Which was almost exactly what Jakob said: Scrolls does not work well in its alpha stage. The risk with letting players in at this early stage is that they judge the game after the first encounter, even though it changes and is improved every week.

However, towards the end of the year it started to become apparent what Jakob was aiming for: a rather fast game that is easy to get started with. Sometimes Jakob refers to Scrolls as a "dumbed down" card role-playing game.

"I simply mean that we've tried to simplify things, a lot of knowledge shouldn't be needed to start playing. We've also lowered the layers of complexity. It takes strategy and planning to be good, but not on so many levels as there are in a lot of other turn-based games. There is not a sea of rules to get through before getting your hands on it."

The reason why it is so dumbed down is simply because Jakob wants it like that.

"I miss the kind of games that has everything that is fun about the games genre, but isn't insanely complicated. I like games that have that element that makes you caught up in it, but where the threshold to start playing is not so damn high."

Even if no one knew how Scrolls' sales would look, it was hardly a financial risk for Mojang. With a small group of developers working on it, Mojang did not have to sell that many copies before the project became profitable. And considering the interest surrounding everything Mojang does and that they already had 50 million players registered at the site Scrolls would be available from, early conservative estimates were that the game would sell at least 100,000 copies, and probably a lot more than that. When the game was released in beta in June 2013, it sold 40,000 copies in one day and reached that 100,000 mark in a week's time.

SUITABLE FOR TABLETS

In addition, there are business opportunities available for Scrolls that aren't for Minecraft. Because even if you, according to Jakob, should be able to play your way to all of the game's content, you will also be able to buy new cards. However, it should be cheaper than it is in other games, and, above all, the cards you buy should be worth the money. Not so many crappy cards then. This is for both honorable and practical reasons: honorable because Jakob simply does not want to trick people, practical because with such a small team of graphic artists you do not have time to overproduce collector cards.

"If you look at similar games that exist today, like for example iPhone and iPad games, you can see that they pull in a lot of money. It is a fairly small group that plays, but they are dedicated and are willing to pay for content. It gives an indication that Scrolls can be a very good deal, even if we only sell a few hundred thousand copies," says Carl.

CAN SOMEONE
SAY WOW!

The last day in February 2012, a few weeks before the ZeniMax affair reached its end, it was time to celebrate that Minecraft had sold more than five million copies. It would be a night to remember, and would echo all over the world.

A few weeks before, Jens had proposed to Jenny. She had said yes and they had started planning their wedding.

"We decided on a budget and made a plan for how much we had to save each month to reach it. We also discovered that it's not so much the wedding itself, as it is how many guests you invite that affects the total cost. It was hard; the budget we could afford meant that we couldn't invite everyone we wanted," Jens remembers.

Daniel Kaplan had other concerns. He had moved

from Skövde to Stockholm and had run into the same problem most young people moving to popular big cities do: finding somewhere to live.

"I had stayed on my cousin's couch, but finally I had decided to buy an apartment of my own. I had to borrow money from my parents and relatives," he says.

The financial statements for Mojang's first fiscal year became set in February, about the same time as the five million mark was surpassed. The first year was really one year and three months since Mojang was formed in October 2010. The numbers were impressive and created headlines all around the world: the turnover landed on roughly $80 million. The profit was $11 million, but "only" $9 million would be divided between the three owners Markus, Jakob and Carl.

DRINKS ARE ON ME

On February 29 it was time to celebrate the success. What Carl, Jakob and Markus already knew was that Markus would give away his part of the profit to the employees. Lydia Winters had also been told about this.

"We had been out partying a week earlier and Markus came up to me and said that in a few days you're going to have a lot of money, a *lot* of money. I didn't want to ask anything about it then," she says.

"But the term 'a lot of money' is pretty wide, it can

mean anything. I tried to contain myself but in the end I couldn't, so I asked Carl what Markus had really meant. He then told me and it came as a complete shock. I was already so happy about everything that had happened in my life through Markus and Minecraft, and now this? To be given so much money that it changes your life, maybe even secures your future? Who does that kind of thing happen to? It was amazing, less than two years earlier I was in Florida, not knowing the first thing about Markus and his game. And now this?"

Lydia cannot keep herself from shedding a few tears when she tells the story, even though she has told it numerous times.

Since Markus is a game developer and likes mathematical and logical thinking, the money was divided according to a thoroughly calculated formula. He simply counted all the days each of the employees had worked for Mojang. All days were added to a sum, which was then divided by Markus's share of the profit, some $3.6 million. Then everyone got that sum for each day they had worked there. Those who were hired first, Daniel and Jens, got the most. Those who came in last got the least.

"It speaks volumes of Markus's character, who he is and how he thinks. That was such a perfect way to be fair and generous," says Lydia.

By the evening's dinner, an envelope was waiting for all the employees. They opened the envelopes and looked

Markus Persson says thanks to his fans at MineCon 2012 in Paris. He said thanks to all of Mojang's employees by giving them his part of the company's profit.

wide-eyed at the paper that was in there. On the paper stood the amount of money each person would get.

The room fell silent.

"I had thought about what reactions it would get, what people would say," Carl remembers. "I had pictured so many scenarios in my head, but not this. It became dead silent, you could've heard a pin drop. I thought, but say something, can someone please shout 'wow'; do something."

But for many, it was simply too much to take in.

"I was prepared, so I wasn't shocked then. But to suddenly get tens of thousands of dollars, hundreds of thousands for some, is nothing you're prepared for. You don't know how to react to that."

Daniel started crying.

"Yes, it was very emotional. It was so much money. For me, it also solved a lot of practical problems."

The first person to break the silence was Junkboy, who had worked almost as long as Jens and was one of the big winners, who shouted that tonight's drinks were on him. For Markus the whole thing was a bit confusing. Why is no one tweeting about this? Were they not happy, he asked Lydia.

"I explained that you don't know how to deal with things like this, to get so much money that it changes your life, how do you act then? I asked Markus if it was okay to tweet about it. He said, 'Of course, we tweet about everything.'"

And thus the news started spreading, first via Twitter, then through other online media and the following days in newspapers. Lydia wrote: "Best day. Incredibly stunned still. I can't even believe it. Notch is amazing. So happy for everyone @ Mojang."

At 3:30 a.m., Daniel Kaplan wrote: "Ok, I will go to sleep now. I'm already crying . . . tears in shock and happiness."

THE WEDDING BUDGET THAT BURST

Some magazine calculated that there was an average of $30,000 per person, which is true if you only count those who worked at Mojang when the fiscal year ended. However, there were more when they passed the five million mark. And the money people received also varied a lot. Daniel and Jens got the most, in Jens's case almost exactly $150,000 after taxes.

"I put them in a special account. Then I went to an ATM and took a withdrawal receipt to see the sum. I still have it, but the text has disappeared."

The only luxuries Jens allowed himself were to give some money to his brother and spend some of it on shopping. Not his own shopping of course.

"My sister lives in Australia. She was here and visited with her kids. I took care of the kids and gave her and Jenny $2,000 each to shop for during the day. And then I did what they do in movies, gave them the condition that they had to spend everything. If they had anything left when they came back, I'd take it. It went really well for my sister, she even had to borrow from Jenny."

However, the savings plan for the wedding, which took place in May 2013, was flushed. And the budget burst.

"Yes, it was like it just disappeared. Suddenly money did not put a limit on how many guests we could invite, instead we ran into another problem. We have 130 we want to invite, but the venue isn't big enough. We'll see how we solve that, it's not very simple."

Late on the night that Markus had given away his money, and everyone had been celebrating until the

7
OTHER
EDITIONS

Minecraft Pocket Edition is the edition of Minecraft available for smartphones and tablets. It is difficult to play. I think so. And so does Jens. And just about everyone at Mojang's office. The game is difficult to control since you control it by pressing and dragging your fingers on the screen. It is simply a lot of pressing on a small screen. In addition, the menus are messy.

But kids do not seem to mind.

The first pocket edition was released in the summer of 2011, at the gaming industry's big convention E3 in Los Angeles. Mojang was there with Sony Ericsson who launched the game together with their gaming phone Xperia Play. That was the same E3 where Lydia first met Markus, Carl and the others and landed her job at Mojang.

Against the prevailing trend, Mojang launched a version for Android first, then on iOS for iPhone and iPad. The Pocket Edition sold reasonably well in 2011, but in 2012 things really started to pick up and at the end of the year they were selling about 20,000 copies a day. If you look at the lists of which games pull in the most money on the App Store, Minecraft seems to constantly be in the top five, many times as number one or two. The game costs $6.99, about a fourth of the price for the computer game. It is still a lot of money.

"We underestimated the kids' ability to embrace the game on mobiles, that's for sure. The fact is that we don't really understand the success ourselves. But I think that the future of Minecraft lies there, as a mobile game," says Jens, who in December 2012 took over responsibility for the game design of the Pocket Edition.

The person who has had the main responsibility for the programming is Aron Nieminen who always, and I mean always, wears a hat (of course I have asked him, like the dad I am, if it does not get hot, whereupon he replied that one gets used to it). He also used to work for King and he coded the first, crude version of Candy Crush right before he left to work for Mojang. It is Aron's fault that neither Jens nor Jakob feel that they are that good at programming and that Markus feels as if he does not know math. Aron is in fact the smartest one in the office, that is what everyone says quite openly, and then you should remember that

Sign this, sign that. Notch's autograph is coveted at every gaming event he visits. Since visiting E3 in 2011, Markus has traveled with a bodyguard — not because of safety concerns, just so he's able to move through conventions at all!

Markus is a member of Mensa, an organization for people with high IQs that you need to pass a test to get into. Jens failed the test by only a few points. But when I asked Jens about his programming skills, he points to Aron.

"If I was really good I would do it like Aron does it; he would just solve the problem, get straight to it and solve it," he says.

Jakob says, "That isn't true, that Jens isn't good I mean. But Aron is perhaps in a league of his own. I'm not at all in the same division as either Jens or Aron. Or Markus for that matter. I'm really not that good."

Markus does not admit defeat when it comes to game programming, but he does in math. "I understand the principles for how math works, but when it comes to really knowing I'm not even close to Aron."

When Aron hears about this, he says, "I'm just like them, I'm not that good either, really."

Which makes Daniel Frisk sigh deeply and exclaim, "Stop it, you're all good. Say it, you're good, damn it!"

Another time, Carl and I are talking about sports stars and game developers, although I cannot remember how we got there. But we were, or rather I was, trying to draw parallels between really good athletes who can be a bit headstrong and programmers like Markus, who can also be like that. Carl agrees to a point, but says, "There's a huge difference though. You rarely meet game developers who are cocky. In my experience they're all very humble, almost too humble."

You cannot do anything but agree with him.

NO HIDDEN RECIPES

The Pocket Edition is in many ways a stripped-down, or early, version of the computer edition of Minecraft. Jens makes all new developments and designs for that edition, and then the updates slowly seep onto the Pocket Edition with approximately one year's delay. It may sound like the mobile version of Minecraft is rubbish, but that is far from true. It has the same appeal and charm as the original, only it is a lot trickier to control. That is my opinion at least, but apparently not the kids'.

One thing that Jens, the others at Mojang and I find tricky with the Pocket Edition is how you actually craft things in the game. In the computer game there are no recipes for anything. You create things with your own imagination — or after looking at YouTube or wikis. Take sand and put it in the furnace and you get glass. Take wood and let it get charred in the furnace. Then take some more wood and first make planks and then sticks out of the planks. Then take a stick and a piece of charcoal and you have a torch.

You create things by placing them in a grid. One of Markus's basic ideas was that people would be allowed to play with the recipes by themselves (but on the other hand, as mentioned before, he did not have time to make a good manual either, and when the fans quickly started to exchange recipes with each other there was no reason to make one). You have a workbench and a furnace, then you have an inventory where you put the things you gather. There is limited space in the inventory, and when you get too much, you cannot collect more. Then you have to put things in a chest before you can gather additional items. There is also a big menu where you can see both the things that can be used for manufacturing and production and the grid where the things can be placed to turn them into something you want, for example a door, a window, a pickaxe, a sword or a fishing pole.

In the pocket edition, it does not really work like that.

It gets too hard even for the kids' dexterity. Scroll menus filled with options are opened instead. If you have the things needed, like a stick and some charcoal, you automatically get the option to make a torch. It takes away a bit of the discover-by-yourself aspect, but the game simply would not work on mobiles in any other way. You are still free to build whatever you want in the game.

The tricky scroll menus are one of the first things Jens set out to fix.

"We may have to add more types of workbenches than we have in the computer version. There you have one workbench for everything, maybe there has to be different workbenches for different materials in the pocket edition. It could be a way to lower the almost infinite number of choices we have in the menus now," he says.

Whoever wants to try mobile Minecraft can download the free version. It gives you a quick feeling of the game.

OUTSOURCING TO DUNDEE

When Mojang, in the summer of 2011, agreed with Microsoft to make a version of Minecraft for Microsoft's game console Xbox 360 they chose a different route. They simply put the production at a different studio, 4J Studios in Dundee. That was the game Daniel Kaplan was preoccupied with when we met in January 2012.

Carl Manneh at Mojang's office in the summer of 2012, with Markus visible just behind Carl to the left.

It resembles the Pocket Edition in its structure; the game is about one year behind the computer edition and has significantly more instructions in it. It is partly because the console players expect more help than the computer players, and partly because it is hard to use all the information online if you are not playing on the computer.

"I always have wikis and forums available when I play. I have to switch between them often to get tips and find out how to do things. It's a natural way of playing for many, I think. But you can't do that when playing Xbox, it's too complicated," says Mojang's analyst and statistics specialist Patrick Geuder.

There were many reasons Mojang put the production on someone else. First and foremost, Mojang does not have enough staff to make that edition too, which demands a bigger team than the one person (Aron) working on the Pocket Edition. But also because they do not want to deal with some of the procedures that come with publishing a game on Microsoft's console. A company like Mojang and the giant Microsoft are not the most obvious pairing.

"Mojang wants to do things their own way. That's when they are at their best. The problem is that it doesn't work like that when you deal with a giant company like Microsoft. There will always be a point where you have to do as they say, end of story," explains Alex Chapman who dealt with a lot of the negotiations on this deal too.

"That's why it was a smart decision to let an entirely different studio take care of the development and a lot of the daily contact with Microsoft. It lets Mojang continue being Mojang."

LUXURIOUS AGREEMENT WITH MICROSOFT

4J Studios are no strangers when it comes to this; they have taken several other well-known game titles to the Xbox 360 throughout the years. Therefore they know both how games should be made to work the best possible way on the Xbox and they also know everything about the tedious approval and test procedures Microsoft has.

How different the business cultures are at Mojang and Microsoft also becomes apparent when I try to interview someone at Microsoft about the whole thing. There are rumors in the industry that the reason Microsoft was so eager and early in trying to get Minecraft in the first place was that Steve Ballmer's kids were huge fans. Hoping to find the truth I sent an email to someone who works with Xbox Live, as the digital marketplace where Minecraft is sold is called. First he says hello and how fun; then, when I ask for a phone interview, I am declined and told to send my questions by email. The reason is to avoid problems. When I then send the questions, I never get a reply.

One of the unique aspects of the deal Mojang gets, and which is quickly picked up on by some other indies, is that they get to update their game more often than other studios. It is an important term, since one of Minecraft's pillars is to constantly evolve.

"It was a classic win-win situation," says Alex Chapman. "Microsoft got exactly what they wanted. They got a game that sells a lot of copies and where they earn money on every copy that is sold. But also, perhaps most importantly, they got millions of young players who spend their time online on Xbox Live. They are satisfied, Mojang is satisfied and I'm satisfied."

The game was finished already in March 2012, but

Microsoft did not want to release it until they had marketing and support ready, and that is why the date was moved to May instead.

Many were skeptical about having Minecraft on Xbox 360. They all knew before it was released that it would be an old version of the game, and they were also afraid that it would be a too simplified version of their beloved game. But it was not. At the website Metacritic, where they gather scores from a number of the world's game sites and game magazines, the computer edition of Minecraft has the impressive score of 93 out of 100. It is basically as close to a perfect score as you can get. Minecraft: Xbox 360 edition has 82. That is also a great score.

In December, game business site GamesIndustry even put it on their list "12 Games that Defined 2012" with the following words: "Just when you thought Minecraft was really, truly a PC phenomenon it turns up on Xbox Live [. . .] and conquers it [. . .] You can bet the success of Minecraft [. . .] is having a massive influence on Microsoft's digital strategy for its next Xbox."

And no matter what the journalists and critics thought, the players loved it. The game was released May 9 and the day after I had an interview with Jakob about Scrolls. On the voice recording you can hear Carl Manneh enter through the front door. He says hi and interrupts the interview by asking if I have heard about the sales numbers from the first day. No, I say and he says that it is already clear that Minecraft set a new sales record for the premiere sales on Xbox Live and the exact figures will arrive in about a half hour. Sure enough, Manneh pops up on the tape just over a half hour later and announces that the figure is 404,000 sold in 24 hours. Daniel Kaplan then adds that they made a profit on the project only an hour after the release. Five days later, the game had sold one million copies (also a record), a month later two million (they then set a new record for total sales) and in July they passed the three million mark. Before the year ended, five million games were sold on Xbox Live.

In the fall, Minecraft became the most played game online on Xbox. For a while it even had more players than the hugely popular soccer game FIFA 13, even though the latter had just been released. It was not until the bestsellers Halo 4 and Call of Duty: Black Ops II were released that Minecraft lost the top position.

LOOK,
I MADE A
MISTAKE

There is another universe parallel to ours, one where the space race never ended. In fact, space exploration once was so accessible that it became popular with wealthy companies and individuals. But in 1988, something went horribly wrong. A new type of cell for deep sleep was released, a cell compatible with every 16-bit computer.

Unfortunately, there was a design flaw with the computers controlling the sleeping cells, a flaw that made everyone in the cells sleep until the year 281 474 976 712 644. When people then slowly started waking up, they awoke to a universe on the brink of extinction, a universe where the black holes were many and energy scarce. This is the set up for 0x10c, Markus's new creation that was made public in March 2012. The actual sequel to Minecraft. Or as Jakob put it: "The difficult second album."

In the beginning, Markus did not reveal exactly how 0x10c should be pronounced; people had to figure it out themselves. But of course, it did not take more than a few minutes before someone came up with an answer. It turned out that the mathematical formula it represents can be pronounced something like "ten to the see." The number also has its own name, Trillek. But it seemed to be "ten to the see" that stuck, at least at Mojang's office. I have heard Jakob say "Trillek" and Patrick "zero x ten c," but other than that they all referred to it as "ten to the see." Markus himself claimed that you could call it whatever you like.

The explanation to the title is as following: $0x10^c$ is a mathematical formula, which makes no sense to me, that programmed the cell to keep people sleeping until the year 281 474 976 712 644.

Simply put, in this game Markus was to move from labors of the earth, to labors in space. If you know the history of video games, it is yet again not a surprising step; science fiction has long had a prominent place in the gaming world. "It is a space game with space fights, simply because it is 'pew pew fun,'" Markus said in an interview with the website Penny Arcade.

To me, he elaborates a bit: "I did not come up with the idea because I'm that much in to sci-fi, because I'm not.

To me it is more about science; I am fascinated by space from that point of view. Then I also like the concept of being alone in a gaming world, as you are in Minecraft too, unless you go online of course. And how much more lonely can you get than being in space?"

For the first months, Markus was blogging and tweeting about it. He said that we will be able to build our own spaceships and that the ships would have 16-bit computers onboard that we will be able to program ourselves (and, scarily enough, the computers will also be affected by viruses, and the players will have to repair it themselves). Specifications for the programmable computer were soon published, and you can still read them yourself at the website 0x10c.com, if you want to sit down and work on programs or games for it already. Other things the game promised to include are hard science fiction, abandoned ships full of loot, an advanced financial system and duct tape.

"But I have given up on hard science, I think. In real life, a normal person can only jump, like, 12 inches, and that is not very fun in a game. I also tried to take away gravity, then you could jump longer but all goes very slow. Not very fun either. So the hard science bit has had to get a little looser."

However you look at it, it is in every way an enormous project that Markus undertook.

"I had several ideas I was working on, a few smaller and one big. The big idea was the space game. But in the end I thought that I might just as well take on the big one," he says. But he quickly adds: "It's on the other hand so big that I'll probably have time to work on the small ones in between."

However, Markus's work on 0x10c quickly began to decrease and during the summer of 2012 he stopped working on it completely.

"I think he was hit by a late hangover from Minecraft," said Carl Manneh after the summer.

In addition, Markus and his wife Elin, whom he also met at King, separated. They had been married for a year. Such things take a toll, even though it appears as if he and Elin continued to be good friends.

In the fall he found new strength; it was obvious both on his Twitter feed and in Markus himself. I saw it with my own eyes when Mojang had their housewarming party at the beginning of October. As it turns out, not only does Mojang have game and play day on Fridays, they also make that a formal Friday once a month. Now they were combining their formal game Friday with the housewarming party.

The office was filled with well-dressed guests, a jazz band and the world's best card magician. But Markus himself was almost absent as he walked around in a suit and with a big smile.

"This is what happens when I get going with the programming. I can't turn it off, it's constantly there," he said, apologetic.

A week later he explained things in more detail: "When

I get into coding mode, my head becomes full of problems that need solving. Last Friday I was thinking about the planet rendering, how will it both look good and run fast? And even if I'm not going to code precisely that, I have to do it so that it can be solved later, I can't lock myself in. It is probably 20 things I need to remember, and each of those things has probably got another 20 subtasks that need to be solved. All that was bouncing around in my head. At times like that I could probably be perceived as a bit absent-minded."

Yes, he could.

The game 0x10c differs a lot from Minecraft. Apart from the space environment and the more adult style of the game, the most obvious difference is the famous space battles that will be "pew pew fun." The battles would occur randomly against computerized ships and against ships controlled by other players, even if it seems as if Markus is not planning for that to be something that happens very often. In space battles ships are broken, and in 0x10c everything that is broken would need to be fixed. Which, by the way, also is the reason why gunfights onboard are not recommended.

There would also be a special arena where players can agree to meet to battle each other PVP (player versus player).

There are also a lot of similarities. For example, just like in Minecraft, you have to find resources, but in this

Jens quizzes Vu: "Is it true that you've held every job?" Has he, for instance, ever developed a game? Of course he has — a simple mathematics game for his little brother. Not a paying job, but Jens is still impressed.

case on the planets you visit. Although, it appears as if machines would help you, because Markus says that the 16-bit computer can be used to play games while waiting for the extraction of a mine.

There would also be a lot of building, since you would be able to craft your own ship. Access to energy is scarce, you have to save and adapt the consumption after the different situations that arise. One can also assume that the game would include both an adventure and a building mode, or as it is called in Minecraft: survival mode and creative mode.

Even the graphic style from Minecraft is there, but when looking at pictures it seems considerably nicer than Minecraft's. Which is not that strange considering that Mojang hired the graphic artist Jonatan Pöljö to work full-time with Markus. One of the reasons why Minecraft looks the way it does is that Markus simply did not have time to make it look nicer. Pöljö himself defines the look like this: the style is pixel art meets modern 3-D.

But other than that, 0x10c would not be a new Minecraft.

"As usual, I just try to make games for myself. I don't feel like I'm trying to make a new Minecraft or that the success of Minecraft puts any pressure on me. I do however feel that it's still tempting to make this game the same way I've done before. I don't want that," says Markus.

"The only thing you can know for sure is if you like the game you're making yourself, you can't really tell about anyone else. To start analyzing target groups and adapting the game after that is just too boring. If you're going to make something you can be proud of, you have to ignore even having a target group."

IN THE FLOW

Markus often talks about being in the flow. He wants to make short interviews, preferably not longer than a half hour for that specific reason. If we ever went on for longer than that, the flow was lost.

"When things are going well, it's fun to program just for programming's sake. When I'm encoding something happens with me, it's something creative. The programming is a tool to create games, that's why I constantly want to learn new things and think about how to solve new problems. Or, I don't really do it to learn new things, I do it so I can make games. There's a difference. You have to, of course, find a balance between flow and hard work. All programming does not demand being creative, not even when you are making games.

"During the Minecraft development it was periods of pretty boring stuff that needed to be done, and after one of those periods I had to force myself back to the flow again. But one of the lessons Minecraft has taught me is that some of the boring stuff is good to get done quickly, even if it isn't a lot of fun. Multiplayer is one of those things. If you start working on it too late, it gives you a lot of extra work, meaning more of the boring stuff."

Another thing Minecraft taught him was to use conventions and clichés.

"I like to put things in the game that tell the players what's ahead. Not to surprise too much is an art form in itself. If you, for example, have a red barrel in a game, it must be able to explode. Cliché is an effective language to use. You can't give too much feedback to the players either; you have to give lots of instant gratification so that the players feel like they're affecting the game."

IT IS A BUG

Even though Markus was tweeting and writing a lot about the game on his blog and the game's website, it was a completely different process compared to how it was with Minecraft. Then he did not start writing publicly about the game until it was playable. The players had the first version of a game that they could give Markus feedback on, which he could then respond to. In the beginning there were not that many players either. It was a small audience. Now it only took a few days before you got tens of thousands of hits on Google when you searched for 0x10c, fan sites quickly started showing up and a 0x10c wiki was started.

And it did not take more than a week before an alternative 0x10c game showed up in the App Store, something that Apple removed when Alex Chapman contacted them. This was another difference compared to the 2009 version of a Notch game: certain basic legal steps preceded it. For example, Chapman had, on behalf of Carl Manneh, investigated and made sure that 0x10c was not a protected trademark; they did not want another ZeniMax affair.

The interest surrounding 0x10c was, in brief, huge, fully in line with when a bigger game studio reveals that they are developing a new game. Both game sites and other media were reporting.

But there was a small catch; there was no game to play for anyone other than Markus and his graphic artist. This meant Markus was only able to inform the fans about the

Jakob Porser between two Scrolls gamers. He and Markus met at King.com, and now they are living their dream, multimillionaires with their own independent game studio.

game rather than having an open dialogue. Because the game was still in such an early stage of its development, a lot of the information was technically advanced. Like the instructions for how to program the 16-bit computer onboard or, for example, this post from the middle of October 2012: "I ran a few tests this week, and at 500 ms latency with 20% packet loss, it seems to be able to handle 1000 packets per second (quite a lot more than it will ever use) indefinitely, which is nice. Of course, I'm ending up reimplementing a lot of TCP, with packet resending and ordering for most things, so I'm not totally sure all this work is actually worth it, heh."

It is not that easy for a mere mortal to understand what Markus was talking about here, even though it is far from the most technical thing that he has written about the game. But there was always that typical openness with his work. Markus wrote about what went right and what went wrong, like in the above where he finished with saying that he is not even sure that the work he had just done will be worth the trouble. When he posted a picture of a piece of source code from the game on Twitter, he discovered shortly afterwards that he had programmed a bug that was visible in the image.

At a big game studio, that would have been a disaster. Or, rather, it would not even happen. First of all, they do not post pictures of the source code. Secondly, every picture that is posted has been thoroughly examined in advance by developers, the PR department and lawyers. There are rules for what can be shown and how many images you need to display. For example, there are always two or three pictures released at the same time from war shooting games where you can see vehicles and weapons. The reason being that if you only show one image you risk being sued by someone who feels that their product, meaning a specific vehicle or weapon, is exposed too clearly. If you have several images, that situation is avoided. And that is just one example.

But Markus sent out a picture of a bug. He quickly corrected his mistake, but not in secret. He did so in full view with the tweet: "Haha, I just saw a bug in that screenshot.

ResendInterval o means it's sending the packets again immediately. Fixed!"

He even pointed out what his mistake was, in case someone had missed it.

But it is not the bugs or the complicated mathematics behind the game that eventually got to Markus. He just didn't have the energy or feeling for the space game he originally envisioned. In 2013, he decided to abandon the project and told all the fans on social media — and that was it. Shortly thereafter, some fans ask to finish the game themselves if it is okay with Markus, which it is. No one yet knows if 0x10c will ever resurface and in what form.

9
TRANSPARENT

This honesty is nearly unique to Markus. There may be others out there who develop games with the same transparency (I have not found them though), but definitely no one with the same amount of attention as Markus gets. Jens, who is the second best at tweeting at Mojang, does not have the same tone in his tweets, even if he does not hesitate to tell you if something goes wrong. Jakob does not even come close.

"I'm really bad with Twitter. I always think that I'll write something, but then I just forget. I could never have the same impact as Markus on a community, not even if I made a successful game like Minecraft. I just don't have his ability when it comes to social media," he says.

Tweeting is the main way Mojang is communicating.

On Mojang's site there are direct links to all the employees' Twitter accounts. Everybody is encouraged to tweet.

"You don't have to be good with social media to work here, that's not what will decide if you are hired or not. But there is no denying it's a big plus. Just be hired by us means you get about 3,000 new Twitter followers," says Carl.

The only person without a Twitter account is Aron. On the other hand, he is the smart one and can probably get away with it.

Markus's openness on Twitter is both spontaneous and planned. For example you cannot find anything on there about his kid, his ex-wife, the divorce or any other too personal details. He simply chooses his own way.

"I want it to be a mixture of silly jokes, some personal things, critique and comments about the game industry and my own programming. All bits need to be there for it to be balanced. If I don't work on any game I often tweet less, because then it becomes too much else there, an unbalance. Everything needs to be there," he says.

It is almost as if he plays the character Notch online.

"Yes, I guess you can say that. But what is a role and what is reality? If you pretend to be social one night and act accordingly, are you then just pretending or are you social for real? Where's the line? Even roles have a tendency to become real and we often play different roles in life anyway," he says.

"But the thing is, I'm fundamentally not an open

person. I'm a geeky person who has been thrown into this. A good thing with the internet is that it has made it a lot easier for people like me to be seen and heard. You could say that Notch is a more official version of myself."

NOT SHY IN THAT WAY

This transparency with everything that is work related has made its mark on the rest of Mojang's staff. Even if there are three part-owners who founded the company together, there is no doubt that it was Markus who made it possible. Therefore his opinions and habits carry more weight, it is just the nature of things. There is simply no denying that it was his game that brought in the big money. "Everyone is aware that Markus is the one who started all this, that he's the reason we can do this," says Jakob.

Furthermore, Markus is a rather stubborn man with strong principles.

"I really haven't met anyone who has such strong views as him. He definitely has a social shyness, but he is not at all shy in that way," says Carl.

The fact is that Markus can almost be devastatingly honest.

"I've been in meetings with Markus where he says things so bluntly it almost makes you gasp for breath, in a way where people could get hurt. But Markus is always like that, honest and straight. When you get used to it it's nice

An introverted star meets his introverted fans. At MineCon, fans line up for the half-hour Q&A with Markus. When time is up, there are still people in line.

because he's always the same, there's nothing false about him. What you see is what you get," says Lydia.

That both Markus and Mojang are so transparent was also one of the reasons why Vu Bui decided to move to Stockholm from L.A., which for a Swede can seem like a strange move, to leave warmth, sun and beaches for a country with a freezing and dark autumn and winter? The fact that his girlfriend, Lydia, had already moved helped, of course, but the transparency was a big factor too.

"I already have my entire life online. That Mojang works the same way suits me perfectly," he says.

Vu tells about his two girlfriends before Lydia. Together with the second to last, he envisioned a project where he would take a picture of her every day for a year and then post it online. Unfortunately the relationship ended after a month, so it only ended up being around 20 pictures. Then he met a girl where their entire relationship was online.

"We showed everything, from meeting online, to the first few dates and then our lives. We even broke up online. To me it's a way of living. It makes me live an honest life, I have to stay true to myself that way. That's what I like so much about Mojang, that this transparency is there and we're allowed to say whatever we want on Twitter or blog about it. I love it. It keeps the company honest."

To me the whole thing feels a bit strange; I have a hard time seeing the obvious connection with being true to oneself and showing your entire life on social media. That is why I sometimes found myself in awkward situations, like when Markus did not have time for our interview but at the same time did make room to post tips on how to make a delicious sandwich online.

Or like when I interview him in December 2012, the last interview of the year actually, and we discussed this very topic, Twitter and growing his almost alternative persona, Notch, online. Later that day I saw that he had written a long blog post just before we met, a sad and beautiful piece about his dad who committed suicide almost exactly one year before. He did not mention it during the interview, and I did not ask since I had not read the post at that point. There was nothing weird in him not bringing it up, but it still gave a feeling of there being almost two parallel worlds; while we were doing a rather personal interview, the only interview that day, maybe for the entire week, there were hundreds of thousands people reading his innermost thoughts about his dad, his dad's addiction and how he shot himself — detailed under the title "I love you, dad."

That blog post, by the way, seems to be the exception to Markus never writing about his family or the really private things online. Perhaps he was able to do it just because his father was dead and that way Markus's words did not violate his privacy? I do not know the reason; I have just noticed that Markus is nearly notoriously respectful in that regard.

IT CAN RUIN THE WHOLE DAY

If you feel like it, you can put this book down for a bit and check out Markus's Twitter feed for yourself — @notch. Even if the frequency of his tweeting varies, chances are that you will find brand new comments about all sorts of things. If you happen to have a Twitter account, you can reply to his tweets and at least have the chance at direct contact with him.

"I like Twitter because it's so easy and simple. There are not many words allowed per tweet and you always have your cellphone at hand. I can take it out on the subway or now, when we're sitting here, and write something. It's very simple to do and very direct. I like it. I don't have time to visit forums like I used to and I very rarely write on my blog," says Markus.

But having over a million followers has its consequences. A lot of people want Markus to tweet about their video game or YouTube channel. A tweet from Notch about a game or a website often gives such dramatic effects that the servers crash, and of course it increases both sales and exposure. The phenomenon even has its own name in Minecraft circles: to get "notched." But Notch runs a hard and clear line: he only tweets about what he wants to tweet, never about anything else. Jeb has the same attitude.

This does not stop Markus from occasionally being controversial. He has tweeted posts that might be perceived as supportive of piracy and he has thrown harsh criticism at the biggest American game publishers.

"Sometimes I'm afraid that having a million followers on Twitter makes me censor myself, but I hope not. It probably wouldn't be a good thing," he says.

He is not only met with love on Twitter. It is for him like for everyone else online; the haters speak louder than the lovers. By the end of 2012, it was reaching levels that made him concerned.

"No matter what I write now, there are people that disagree. And they are often the ones who reply. Sometimes

No one knows the exact demography of Minecraft gamers, but it's safe to say young males dominate the scene.

it's okay, you can have a difference of opinion and those who respond might have a point in what they say. But often it's just mean, or they give me crap for things I don't have anything do with," he says.

"It's often young people who are mean just for the fun of it. If I reply I often get an apology. But now I usually don't bother, I just block them straight away, almost automatically. It works for me, it makes me feels as if I've at least done something to solve the problem. I've also discovered that the negative and positive comments come in clusters. So another tactic I have is to find the positive and read them after I've read the negative ones. Then it usually feels better again."

What Markus does not want, but what he is afraid might happen, is that he will stop reading the replies to his tweets.

"To read the replies can ruin my day. I can't deal with that. If I don't come up with a better strategy I might have to stop reading them altogether. Then my tweeting will become more of a monologue. It might happen that way, but I hope not."

IN THE HEADS OF CARMACK AND ROMERO

Before 0x10c was shelved, the original plan was to get more programmers to help Markus with the game, somewhere in between the alpha and beta stages perhaps. That would have been a completely different process than with Minecraft.

"I'll work on it by myself until I think the game is fun, and then we'll bring more developers in. Right now so much of it is only in my head," said Markus. "It's hard to bring in others, it's easier to just do it myself."

This might be different from how Markus did it last time, but not different from how things were done in the early days of game development, in the '80s and early '90s.

"Then the games were often made by teams with between one and five people, not more. When you keep the teams that small, you can still make games that are personal. Doom was made by about that many, and it's a very personal game."

In the end of October 2012, Markus shows a short video of the multiplayer mode in 0x10c. It is actually striking how similar it looks to Doom. This is not a coincidence.

The year was 1993 and Id Softworks, a bunch of American youngsters led by John Carmack and John Romero, had cobbled together a game that would become a classic and a milestone in the gaming world. They sat, just like Mojang, in an apartment (but in Texas, not in Stockholm) and sold their games directly to the players through so-called shareware, where you got to play the first few levels for free but paid to play more. What Romero and especially Carmack had succeeded with was to create advanced 3-D physics in a very fast game.

The player saw the world through the character's eyes, called first person view. You simply look into the gaming world as if you were the protagonist you play. You see nothing more of the protagonist than the hand or the weapon in the hand. The story in Doom is simple: you are the only surviving marine who has to fight against a large number of monsters and demons in a science fiction environment. Doom gave birth to the genre that is called FPS, which stands for first person shooter. It is fair to say that today's blockbusters Call of Duty and Battlefield are direct descendants from Doom.

Just like millions of other teenagers around the world, Markus sat wide-eyed in front of his computer and shot his way through the dark, violent and fun game worlds that the young Americans had created. But already back in 1993 it was much more than an adrenaline rush for him.

"To me, it was like stepping right inside their heads, straight into Romero's and Carmack's minds. It was as if I saw a little bit of them, of their way of thinking," remembers Markus.

At night, he dreamt of the game. There were surely many other teenage boys who did the same thing. Yet, they probably did not dream about it in same way as Markus did.

"I dreamt that I was the one who programmed the game engine for Doom. That it was I who made it work. I still dream that kind of dreams, but where I used to dream that I programmed the games, I now dream more about me designing them."

Markus simply could not play Doom without thinking about how Carmack and Romero had done it, how they had programmed and designed the game for it to be as fun and technically advanced as it was. He spent just as much time thinking about that as he did playing the game.

Just like he could see Carmack and Romero in Doom, Markus wants you to see something of him in Minecraft. But do not expect any stories.

"No, I'm no storyteller, I don't have that many stories

to tell. To me, it's about creating experiences or letting the players create their own stories. Maybe I have a few stories I'd like to tell in the future, but that's not where my strength lies. At least I don't think so; it's not like I've actually tried."

Markus believes that Minecraft says more about him than 0x10c.

"Yes, 0x10c is not a game like that to me. There might be a feeling that is me, but not so much. It's personal in other ways, it's, just like Minecraft, my own game."

Not only does Twitter work as a way to communicate with fans and media for Markus, it has also become a way to make and keep friends all over the world, some of them still surprising to Notch himself. For example, Peter Molyneux is there, the man who designed Dungeon Keeper, a game that still is a big favorite of Markus's and an inspiration for Minecraft. Molyneux is, by the way, one of the few people Markus has ever asked for an autograph.

But more importantly, John Romero is there. Markus says that they are friends on Twitter, and just saying it seems to give him goose bumps.

"We've met and we clicked instantly. When it comes to game design it feels as if we are thinking the same way. But it's weird when he says that I'm an inspiration to him, that what I have done has affected how he thinks about making games. It almost feels wrong, like hello, you're

John Romero who made Doom. But of course it's fun. And it's very nice to have such easy and direct communication via Twitter."

And, of course, anyone who is interested can read what Notch and Romero tweet about with each other.

THIS
IS WHAT
WE ARE

In June 2012, one week after Markus's birthday and two days after Carl Manneh and his wife had a baby, Mojang moves into their new quarters, maybe a 15 minute walk from the old apartment. The office is decorated like a British gentlemen's club. The idea came from Markus, who claimed that it ended up being that because all the other ideas were shot down. The architectural firm wrote about their vision for the office: "Everything started with a story about the fictional character Sir Mojang, who he is, what his characteristics are and what he does when no one is looking."

Apparently Sir Mojang likes thick plaid carpeting and English leather couches. He plays pool and pinball. He wants a kitchen island in the middle of the office, a long, rustic dinner table in the middle, with several small and one big meeting room, the latter with a globe hiding whiskey and cognac bottles. He wants a game room as big as a small movie theater and a small hideout furthest in the back.

A little while after they moved, Mojang's coat of arms was hung up on the wall. It was, like most things, designed by Junkboy. In the part of the office where the couches and pool table are, they also put up oil portraits of employees. The portraits were ordered from India and arrived at the beginning of 2013. Of course, not every employee is represented by a portrait, since the workforce has increased since the summer of 2012 but the available wall space for portraits has not similarly grown.

There is, however, ample space for more employees than the 26 that work here already.

"First we drew the line at eight employees, we would definitely not be more than that. Then it was 15, but that didn't work either. Now I believe we're thinking 30, not more," says Jakob.

Carl draws the line at what the venue can accommodate.

"We could be 35 or 40 people here, not more. But today it looks like we only need two or three more, that should be it," he says.

SMALL GROUPS

Even though Fridays are research days at Mojang, it is not always fun and games. People actually work hard. It

Jakob Porser takes in the view at Disneyland Paris. His game Scrolls is actually Mojang's first game, since Minecraft was published before the studio started.

is not easy to avoid your job assignments, if by any chance you would want to do that. For an indie game developing studio, a staff of 26 is a lot, but not so many that anyone goes unnoticed. On the contrary. Everyone has their own clear assignments and no game is so big that more than a handful of people are working on it. In 2012, Jens made Minecraft, at the end of the year with the help of Nathan Adams. No one else. Then there were others working with server functions and the new interface for how players could add their own things to the game. But even those areas were handled by one or only a few people. When I asked about the progress of a particular project, I always got the answer that this or that person had gotten this or that far. Everything was personal and clear. That is how it has been ever since Markus first showed Minecraft; it was one game and one person responsible for it. For Markus it is almost a matter of principle.

"I say it all the time, I like video games that have been made by only one or a few people. I make games the same way. I want to express something, a feeling or maybe just a game mechanic or a design solution that is my own. In my eyes, such things can be beautiful; it doesn't even need to be recognized by the players, it's enough if I think it's a beauty."

That remained the guideline for how to do games at Mojang, even if there no longer were any one-man teams. The biggest group at the office was working with Scrolls, and it consisted of four to six people, depending on what day and how you look at it. It was a record in size that no one at the office wanted to beat in the future. With Mojang's standards, it was a huge project.

Then you should take into consideration that there could be anything between 50 and 300 people working at a so-called triple-A game, the most expensive productions in the gaming world. When Dice makes a new Battlefield game, a typical AAA-title, anywhere between 100 and 250 developers are working for two or three years with that single game. But even studios in Mojang's size often work in larger groups. The newly started Scattered

Entertainment, a studio owned by the Japanese mobile games giant DeNA, has their office close to Mojang. They have about the same number of employees as Mojang, but they are all working on one and the same game. What is considered big at Mojang is therefore small compared to other game studios, at least those who make any money.

This way of working not only means that each person at Mojang has a lot of work on his or her hands; it is also up to them to get it done. There is no one to hide behind. Sometimes I have been sitting at that long dinner table, while waiting for an interview to start, and just observed and listened. There are no snowball fights going on and no one is drinking expensive whiskey. People are working quietly and are persistently studying their computer screens. Diligence was the word that came to mind.

MONDAYS AT THE DINNER TABLE

In the early days of Mojang, in the fall of 2010 and spring of 2011, there were so few people working at Mojang that most things could be taken care of through informal meetings. A handful of guys who all loved video games, and who worked side by side, simply did not need any scheduled meetings to be updated about each other's work. They even had lunch together every single day. To avoid discussions about where they would go to eat, Jens solved the whole thing by making a mini game; he built a random lunch generator. All the restaurants they usually visited and new ones that were discovered were written into the program. Before they left the office, they pressed a button on the computer and a restaurant immediately came up.

Today they no longer organize common lunches, but the majority of the Mojangstas still sits at the long dinner table and eats together anyway.

What everyone has done the past week and will do the next is reported in a casual way every Monday at 9 a.m. Then they all gather at the dinner table to talk about what is happening right now at work. It is not done with PowerPoint presentations or anything like that; each and every one simply reports, in their own words, if they have reached the goals that were set up last week, and what new goals are set up for the coming one.

"This way of communicating creates a positive peer pressure. If you stand up in front of a group and tell them what you are going to do, then you also have an obligation to the group to deliver. I think that's the best form of organization you can create as a manager, to get the team to organize themselves and set their own goals," says Carl.

The open dialogue is vital, means Markus. That it is an appealing and open spirit is so critical that he, Jakob and Carl always take that in to consideration when they meet potential new employees.

"We haven't managed to form any strategy for what kind of personnel we should employ; we simply just look at who is the best fit. The most important thing is that we don't hire people who are all the same. It's both about people's competence and their personality, the atmosphere at the office is so important to us. It can neither be too boring nor too silly, you need a balance," he says.

"People must be allowed to have opinions about everything, from high to low. When everyone feels as if they can have an opinion and that their voice is heard, then you get the best of both worlds. Mojang brings out the most and best of everyone that works here, and people enjoy working here."

Within the teams you communicate, of course, more than on Mondays, but doing so does not need any special organization.

Or as Vu Bui puts it: "I'm hired as the operations manager, but there really are no operations to manage that way, at least not when it comes to the games we're doing. The teams are so small that it'd just be silly to manage them. Each team is self-propelled," he notes.

BEING "INDIE"?

That only one or a few people work on entire games felt like something new and fresh in the gaming industry when Mojang got started. The triple-A studios seemed to dominate the scene, but already before Mojang started, the indie scene had started to explode. One of the main reasons for that was, of course, the possibility to self-publish games online. Indie developers could either do it as Markus had, via their own site, or via a game portal like Valve's Steam. What it meant was that there was no publishing house wanting a share of the profit, nor were there any costs for printing and distributing a game. There was also a demand from gamers for smaller, more personal games, like Minecraft.

Today the indie scene is vibrant and growing as never before. It is mainly from the indies that new ways of doing games, and perceiving what games are and can be, originate. And almost every indie game is made by one or just a handful of developers. In other words, it is much like the way indie music was once the term for musicians and bands that chose not to sign with the major music labels to be able to do their own thing. But just like in music, where it became more of a collective term for a certain kind of music, the indie concept in the gaming world is already changing. And Mojang is at the forefront.

Already when Mojang received awards at the annual indie game festival in 2011, people started muttering. When Mojang got better conditions than other small studios with Microsoft for the launch on Xbox Live, they muttered even more. When Markus, on Twitter, attacked the big publisher Electronic Arts when they tried to mooch on the word "indie" for a launch, he felt compelled to also point out that he no longer considered Mojang being indie.

On the other hand, it is obvious to everyone that

Markus smiles in his fedora hat, which has become somewhat of a trademark.

Markus, Jens and the others almost personify the term indie. Indie as in independent. Both in how they act and in how their games look and are designed. You simply cannot make too big, complex and graphically beautiful games when you work in as small groups as Mojang does. So even if Mojang is rich, they still make games that look every bit as indie as any other indie game out there. They also do exactly the games they want to do; they kept going on Scrolls and 0x10c instead of investing in Minecraft 2. Mojang is in that way almost more free and independent than other indie studios, just because they can afford it.

"The term indie is so strange. Is indie being poor? Is indie being just one or two persons? Or is indie just being independent from the big publishers? It can be neither of that I think. To imply that a huge company like Valve is indie is just stupid, even though they clearly are independent. To me it sometimes seems like there are a few persons out there that have tried to hijack the term indie," says Jakob, who, on the other hand, claims he never understood the term to begin with, even when they founded Mojang.

TO SAY NO. AND YES.

Be it as it may, Mojang is ready to go far to keep that freedom and independence. For example, Mojang strives to be an open and transparent company with as few secrets as possible. During my year with Mojang, I am only told about three things that I have to keep quiet about. Two of them are temporary secrets because negotiations are still ongoing; they would soon become public. One is secret-secret. It is about the game project that Mojang revealed to their fans at the end of 2011. It was thwarted. Or rather: Markus, Jakob and Carl decided to shut it down, even though they had put in a lot of money and time on the project. The reason for that? They were not able to develop the game exactly as they wished.

"It didn't come down to anyone being dissatisfied with the game or that the project was bad, we just couldn't get our way of doing things to work with how the partner needed to do it. The only way to move on with the game had been for us to adapt to their way of running the project. We had long discussions about it, but in the end we decided to shut it all down. It's just not the way we work; it wasn't what we wanted when we started all this," says Carl.

It was not an easy decision. Patrick Geuder still swears loudly over the fact that it did not happen and Carl can barely resist pointing out what a shame it was that it had to be closed down.

Which still did not prevent Mojang from doing the occasional debauchery during the year. Like when Lego considered making a piece of Minecraft Lego. Not such a strange idea when you think about it; Minecraft has often been described as a form of digital Lego. That is no coincidence; Lego was, next to computers and programming, Markus's big interest when he was a child (and anyone who follows him on Twitter might have noticed that he still buys the odd Lego kit to assemble just for the fun of it). Lego has a website where people can post their own suggestions for future Lego kits (lego.cuusoo.com if you are interested). There they had planned on showing Minecraft Lego as a suggestion, and then the Lego fans would be able to vote for what model they wanted produced. A suggestion needed at least 10,000 votes in order for it to get on a list that was then taken under consideration by a special committee. For Lego, this was a way to get new ideas that were already popular with the biggest Lego fans.

The people in charge of the website were in agreement with Carl on the project; they saw the obvious potential in combining Lego with Minecraft. But there was another level of executives that needed convincing. So Carl and Daniel Kaplan went to Lego's headquarters right at Legoland in Denmark.

The executives liked the idea, but were not completely convinced. Carl and Daniel had discovered, though, that there were already several suggestions for Minecraft Lego on the website. Curious to see how the Minecraft fans would react, Daniel tweeted about it and added the link to the site.

It crashed instantly.

So many members of the Minecraft community had clicked their way to the Lego site that it simply did not hold for the onslaught. The Lego executives excused themselves and contacted the IT department, and soon the site was up and running again. Then Daniel tried tweeting again. With the same result. The site crashed.

"It became an odd meeting. On one hand, they were very impressed by the power of our community. On the other, they probably felt a bit embarrassed that their site couldn't handle the traffic," says Carl.

The next day, the people at Lego contacted them again. The website was now fixed and improved, Mojang should feel free to once again direct the community to the Lego site. This time Daniel wrote about the project on Mojang's Facebook site.

And for a third time, the website crashed.

"After that, they were pretty convinced that a Minecraft Lego was a good idea," says Carl and laughs.

The Minecraft Lego was launched during the summer. It quickly sold out. In the U.S., the demand was so high that the magazine *Forbes* wrote about it, because there was no Minecraft Lego left to buy for the Christmas season.

MINECRAFT, THE MOVIE

Even though Daniel Kaplan was part of that process, he is doubtful whether Mojang should really do things like the special Lego. It is a fun project, no doubt, but Kaplan's take on things is very straightforward: Mojang should make games, and as little else as possible.

Carl agrees, and so do Markus and Jakob, even if they are more compromising than Daniel.

"We do say no to many of the suggestions we get, most of them actually. It's not necessarily because they're bad, it's just that they don't suit us or they take away the focus from what we're supposed to be doing," says Carl.

Not all suggestions can be ignored, though, no matter how far from game production they are. Like when one of Hollywood's hottest film agents contacted them with an idea for Minecraft the movie. She was not the first to come with a suggestion like that, but her idea was to make a darker film and she, by her own admission, knew the Dark Knight Trilogy director Christopher Nolan. The agent visited just in time for Mojang's housewarming party. Since the whole thing was unexpected and also a bit glamorous, I took the opportunity to say hello. She said hi back, and there she was, a real life Hollywood agent. She was not the only one interested, there were more. Behind them were companies like Columbia and Warner, showing interest. Minecraft's loyal fan base and the 50 million players were of course presumed moviegoers. Even if there is a long way to go until there actually is a movie, it is also far from just being a fantasy project.

"But we understand that it's a long shot. It can go either way, it can be the red carpet in Hollywood or it can be nothing. But it's worth a shot anyway," says Carl.

It is worth noting that Minecraft the movie would not be an animated movie but a live action one. But it can, as Carl says, go either way.

NO PUBLISHER

Then there was that pet project that even Daniel Kaplan wanted to do — helping other indies. One of Markus's dreams when starting Mojang was to give other, less fortunate indie developers a helping hand.

There were many ideas about it throughout 2012,

including thoughts about how Mojang could use the large base of Minecraft players to launch indie games widely through a special downloading portal. A bit like Valve's Steam, but only for indies. There were also plans on letting other indie developers work out of Mojang's new office. That was the idea Daniel Kaplan spoke of when we met for the first time in January.

After moving to the new offices, Carl and the others realized that they had been way too optimistic about that. There really is not as much space as they had thought, and even less time to help others. Oxeye is the exception; they had been working out of Mojang's premises for a while, they kind of came together with Jens. Mojang also has a publishing deal with Oxeye and were promoting their game even before my first meeting with Daniel. Oxeye operates essentially as a part of Mojang.

"It was a hard decision, but we had to ask ourselves a tough question: should we devote our time to publish other developers' games, or should we make our own unique games? We came to the decision that it's the latter, we should focus on making our own games," says Carl.

Alex Chapman agrees with the decision.

"I really like that Carl, Markus and Jakob protect [Mojang's] identity. That integrity will get them far. They're not selling themselves to make money in the short term, they don't need to either because they obviously have such a good economy. As long as Carl, Markus and Jakob continue to be the people they are and own the company themselves, I think that Mojang will remain the company it is today," he says.

The thought of publishing the games of others is not entirely abandoned, though. They have decided on one condition: if they publish a game made by another indie, it needs to be a bit like Markus's game. Mojang needs to be able to sell it in alpha and beta editions before releasing it. Projects like Scrolls are only to be done in-house. At least that is the ambition — Markus speaks of it often enough for the dream to stay alive — but with everything happening with Mojang at such a fast pace, it is very difficult to predict the future.

A KNIGHT FOR THE INDIES

There is, however, no doubt that Markus is passionate about indie developers. He frequently invests in Kickstarter projects.

Kickstarter is the first and biggest site that devoted itself to what is called crowd funding. It is based on letting authors launch their products on a website to try to entice the public to finance it. Instead of trying to find investors that invest a large sum of money in a risky project, you turn, through the internet, to the general public and ask for many smaller investments. Often the projects are too small to attract the truly rich investors anyway. Today there are many more crowd funding sites than Kickstarter, which, however, gave its name to the phenomenon.

In practice, this often becomes a fan-financing thing, whether it is about video games, investigative journalism, movies or anything else. Whoever wants to see a certain project realized pays a sum anywhere between ten dollars and several thousands. They do this both because they believe in the project and, even more so, because they want to see them realized. That is how the documentary *Minecraft: The Story of Mojang*, which was filmed in 2011, was financed. Markus invests, or maybe donates is a more appropriate term, a lot of money on Kickstarter for game projects he finds tempting.

"I give money to games I think seem fun and have some potential, but most importantly to developers I become interested in and believe in. I never finance entire games, but I often give the maximum amount of money that you can donate," he says.

This thing with supporting and encouraging the indies is also a great driving force to arrange all those big and luxurious parties that Markus is known for. There is always a VIP section for indie developers.

"I like the idea of arranging a party with the best music, the best sound, the best VIP section and then inviting the indies there. In my eyes, they are the ones who are the real VIPs."

11
CARL WANTS TO SAVE THE WORLD

One summer's day, Carl Manneh received an email that caught his attention. With an inbox overflowing with propositions from Hollywood, newspapers and TV shows from all over the world, and people like Björn Ulvaeus from ABBA turning up at his door just for a chat, there was not much that surprised Carl anymore. But this was different.

The email came from Tomas Melin, head of the Office of External Relations at the UN-Habitat in Nairobi, Kenya. Even Daniel Kaplan had a hard time saying no.

"Hollywood and all that other stuff is fun, sure. But still, is that something we really should be doing? Everything, even fun stuff, takes time and energy from something else. My firm belief is that we should say no to just about everything that doesn't involve making our games. But, well, this is the UN. It's . . . well, it's the UN. How do you turn that down? It's cool. It's big," he admits.

Carl did not have to think twice about it. "To be able to use Minecraft for humanitarian purposes, I mean, just the thought of it was thrilling. Of course I was curious."

Carl, Jakob and Markus are the three owners of Mojang. One of the few things they do not speak openly about is the amount of shares each of them holds, but it is a fair assumption that Markus and Jakob own between 80 and 90 percent, with Carl as a minority owner. Another way to explain how it all works is this: Markus and Jakob own more than Carl, but Carl runs the company more than Markus and Jakob. Carl makes most of the everyday decisions (in other words, he usually knows what Markus and Jakob think and can say yes or no on his own in most cases), but more important or tricky things are discussed either over dinner or in a quick meeting in the cubicle where Markus and Jakob work. Neither Markus nor Jakob want any part of being boss at the office.

"I'm not the boss. I'm not the head of anything here. Don't write that, I'm not a boss. I don't want that. Carl is the boss, he is CEO," Jakob says. You get the feeling that he almost wants to form a cross with his fingers, like he is protecting himself from a curse.

Of course it is not that simple. Markus and Jakob are not your regular coworkers, not just the guys working on the computers next to yours. It may be that they do not exercise any hands-on leadership or managing at the office, but of course their words carry extra weight. And, as I said, Carl does not make any big decisions without consulting them. Since the owners are also the company's board, a late dinner is the perfect way to handle these questions in a more casual and friendly way.

It was during one of these dinner meetings that the request from the UN in Nairobi ended up being discussed, since it quickly became an important issue to Carl. While Jakob and Markus made video games, he wanted to save a small part of the world.

CHANGING THE HOOD

If you have ever played Minecraft, you know that it is a game of free building. And that is exactly what the UN-Habitat wanted the game for. In Sweden, Minecraft was already being used in large renewal projects in some big cities. An industry organization called Swedish Building Services uses Minecraft to show local citizens the plans for renewal, but also to get their feedback. Minecraft, with its rather crude and not very detailed graphics, turns out to be at an almost perfect level of information for everyone to understand. It is also a very inviting way for ordinary people to show and test their own ideas for what should be done in an area.

"When you see building plans or even real 3-D models of large projects, you'll find that they are often way too detailed. It will, of course, tell you exactly how high a door is or exactly how many inches from the corner it'll be. But who cares, except for the builders? If you live in that neighborhood, all you want to know is that there will be a door in that corner, and roughly where a new house will be built. Minecraft is perfect for that, the level of detail and information is just perfect for these types of project," says Vu Bui.

This is already happening in Sweden, with gamers from the Swedish Minecraft community providing in-game maps of neighborhoods. It is a bit like building a large scale Lego model of the areas, and then providing the citizens with an infinite number of Lego pieces so they can rebuild and change the map to show what they want their neighborhood to look like.

TAKING THE GAME TO THE SLUMS

This is the project that Tomas Melin, also a Swede, had discovered. He also quickly realized that this way of working would suit a project that UN-Habitat was about to undertake to help the poorest big city dwellers in the world.

"They thought Minecraft was a perfect fit. It was very flattering," says Carl.

According to Wikipedia, UN-Habitat is United Nations' agency for human settlements and is mandated to promote socially and environmentally sustainable towns and cities with the goal of providing adequate shelter for all. That is not, as we all understand, a small task. The agency was formed in 1978, when it was becoming clear that the big cities were going to grow explosively all around the world and not least in the developing world. In a project called Block by Block, the UN wanted to renew public areas in 300 of the world's poorest slums and shantytowns in the big cities in developing countries. Furthermore, they wanted to do this in just three years. But they had even higher goals than that; they wanted to do it the right way, meaning finding out what the residents wanted.

"How to interact with people in the poor areas is a problem for decision-makers everywhere, even in rich countries like Sweden. That problem is even bigger in these very poor places. Money is seldom a problem. Often enough there already is money for these projects, but the big question is — what do the people in the slums want? What do they need? How do you engage them in the renewal of public spaces? That's what's hard," says Vu.

The tight time schedule would probably be impossible without Minecraft's greatest asset — the community. When the Swedish project started, Carl tweeted that he needed some good Swedish Minecrafters to help build the maps. Within minutes he had more replies than he could handle.

"Of course, the UN liked Minecraft as a tool to build maps and to get locals engaged, but what they really wanted, what was the key to it all, was our community. That's the power that can carry such an undertaking as this," says Carl.

300 AREAS IN THREE YEARS

Block by Block was planned to resemble its Swedish predecessor. The UN-Habitat is to provide pictures and measurements of the public spaces from the project. Then various groups in the Minecraft community are to replicate them in the game. This will be done for free. It is a huge job to undertake.

Even though Block By Block is somewhat of Carl's own pet project, it did not take him long to convince Markus and Jakob to get onboard. When they all met for their board dinner, it was decided that Mojang would be the project's main sponsor. Not only that, they also decided to give an extra $100,000 to cover things such as travel costs and external services, and the same amount to internal costs, for example letting Vu and Lydia be in charge of the project. As if that was not enough, it was also decided that for the next three years Block by Block would be the main recipient of Mojang's charity work. For Christmas 2012, Mojang worked together with 4J Studios and Microsoft to create a special charity skin pack sale for the Xbox edition of the game, thereby raising over $700,000 for Block by Block. The money is used mainly for computers, training of personnel, infrastructure, broadband connections and other expenses (rather than for the rebuilding of the sites).

In February 2013, Mojang held their now annual Mojam, a weekend-long event where the studio makes experimental games for people who donate money. The donations were split between four charities, Block by Block being one of them. In a move to get more people to donate, Markus promised to shave his beard if they reached $500,000. Of course that goal was reached, and Markus was promptly shaved — the whole thing, of course, filmed and shown on social media.

Block by Block was an ambitious project. "In some areas, there are schools or community centers with computers we can use, like in Nairobi. But I'm sure we'll come across places where everything needs to be fixed. We will deal with that there and then," says Vu.

WHERE WILL THE BULLET HIT?

In early October 2012, Vu took a flight to Nairobi for a first meeting with UN-Habitat. Not only can you find the agency's headquarters in Nairobi, you can also find Kibera there. It is the second largest urban slum in Africa and, partly due to UN's presence, one of the world's best-known slum areas. According to Vu, it houses somewhere between 200,000 and 700,000 people, although a report from 2009 states the population as 170,000. Before that, Kibera was thought to

One of the public spaces in Kibera that is awaiting renewal with the help of Minecraft builders. (The photo is taken by Vu Bui, the Minecraft build is by FyreUK, courtesy of Mojang.)

be home to millions of people, thus being one of the biggest informal urban settings, the more politically correct wording for it, in the world. Vu says that no one really knows how many live there, but that was the figure he was told on site. It is still a lot of people, and the area is dirt-poor. This is where Block by Block's two pilot projects were to take place.

Part of Vu's mission was to show how Minecraft works and follow UN workers and some other personnel to the public spaces up for renewal. There, he was also going to show what measurements and pictures were needed to make a Minecraft version of the place. These would then be sent to the most famous group of Minecraft builders in the world, the British FyreUK.

"The only way to do this is, of course, to go to the place where the pilot is to be done. It's one thing to try and understand the need for this project sitting in a safe environment in Sweden, a different matter to be on the location and see and smell the poverty. We needed to see this," says Vu. Vu got more than he bargained for.

While visiting one of the locations, an open field, together with a group of about 20 people, Vu and some of the others ended up a few steps away from the group. Vu, being from L.A. and all, knows how to act in dangerous neighborhoods, and thought nothing more of the situation. They were close to the rest of the group, they were also in an open field. He figured it was pretty safe.

But as he turned around, a gang of five or six youngsters turned up out of nowhere.

"I remember thinking, where the hell did they come from? I hadn't heard or seen them, but there they were. They were very calm, just looked at us. Then one of the guys took out a gun, an old battered gun that looked like it'd been to hell and back. It was in a terrible state, but still, it was a gun. As he cocked it, I suddenly realized what was happening. Lay down, he told us. I went flat on the ground. No hesitation. The guy with the gun always wins, even if you are a hundred to one. No one wants to take the one bullet he'll be able to fire."

Vu Bui took this picture of himself just minutes before being robbed point blank. (Photo courtesy of Vu Bui.)

In his backpack, Vu had both his computer and his passport. His phone was in his left front pocket.

"It's sounds like a totally stupid thing to do, to bring a passport and a computer to one of the poorest areas in the world. But I needed the computer to show Minecraft and the passport to get into the UN headquarters."

Someone took his backpack, but Vu was able to lean a bit to his left, hoping the guy patting him down would miss the phone, assuming he had already gotten all the important stuff in the backpack. It worked. "But damn, I loved that backpack," says Vu.

It was over in seconds.

"As I lay there with my nose in the ground, I was having some strange thoughts. I wasn't afraid and did not think of death. What I thought of, however, was where the bullet was going to hit, maybe in my head? Or in the neck, or maybe in my back? Then all went quiet and after a short while, I lifted my head very slowly. I saw the gang walking away across the field, very slowly, almost like they were enjoying the weather or something. It was surreal."

It took the rest of the day to just find the right police station to file charges at, which was needed for insurance and a new passport. Vu felt a strange calmness.

"I think it helped that I was facedown during the mugging. One of the other guys hadn't seen the weapon and tried to resist. Someone had hit him, and made him sit down facing the guy with the gun. For him it was more traumatizing. I did not have the same, frightening experience happening in my face."

But when Vu reached his hotel, the fear hit him. Hard.

"Paranoia set in. For the rest of the trip I simply couldn't relax. It was scary, really scary. I was afraid until I stepped off the plane in Stockholm. Then it just disappeared. It's one of many things I love about my new home: Stockholm is such a safe place. I always feel secure here."

Back in Nairobi, Tomas Melin was nervous. The Block by Block project had not gotten off to a great start with its main contributor and sponsor. Would the UN lose

Mojang's partnership before the project even got started? They needn't have worried.

"Was it a scary thing that happened? Yes, very much so. Was it a reason to pull out? No, on the contrary. To me it just proved we were on the right track. Kibera and those kind of places are exactly where we need to be. It just showed to me how great the need is for a project like Block by Block."

There were some consequences, though. When Lydia made the same trip a month later to deliver the maps from FyreUK, she was not allowed to go alone. "It's not a problem for me, but the guys won't let me," she complained to me.

"No way I'm letting Lydia go there on her own, no way," said Vu.

This time around, local guards accompanied them. Everything went fine, but Vu did not enjoy himself.

"No, I was afraid all the time. I just couldn't relax. But still, that's not a reason for us not to get involved."

Things did not turn out well for the young robbers. Vu later found out that they had been on a days-long robbing spree in Kibera. When they had tried to rob a store, they got in a gunfight with a guard. Two of members of the gang were shot dead.

"Before I came here I was more of a hard-lined American, I would've thought they just got what they deserved. But now . . . maybe I'm not feeling sorry for them, but I don't necessarily think that it was a good ending to it all. If you choose the path they did, there will be consequences, but at the same time . . . I don't know really, I don't have a good feeling about it, that's all."

Vu and Lydia barely had time to land in Sweden before it was time for the next strange journey — this time, though, in a much safer and more fun setting. It was time for MineCon 2012.

12
MINECON IN FANTASYLAND

It was a cloudy morning and the drizzle was falling down on me as I walked from Disneyland Hotel towards Hotel New York. I was at Disneyland Paris, the French version of the American fantasyland. That morning, it felt bleaker and more misplaced than ever; it's much better suited to sunny California or Florida than France during the winter, trust me. The only people moving around the two amusement parks were a few early arriving families and some staff, or cast members as everyone at Disney is called. It was around 9 a.m., and I was off to meet Carl at Hotel New York, where he and the other Mojangstas were staying. It was November 24 and the opening ceremony of MineCon 2012 was an hour and a half away.

I had to go with Carl in order to get into the Disney

Events Arena, where there were seats for 7,000 people and still room for shops, a food court and hundreds of computers lined up so the participants could play Minecraft, Scrolls and Cobalt. To call it an arena was somewhat of an exaggeration, since it was more or less a large tent.

The tickets had been released two months earlier. First, Mojang released 5,000 tickets. They sold out in less than 30 minutes. Another 2,000 were released a few weeks later, and they sold just as fast. It was not like Mojang was giving them away for free; each ticket sold for $99. Then you also had to add travel costs, hotel and food. That's why I had thought the French would outnumber other nationalities, but that was not the case at all. English was the dominant language, with most visitors coming from Britain, but also as far away as the U.S. and Australia. There were over 20 nationalities represented. They all had invested a large amount of money to be a part of MineCon. Even though I got the ticket to the event for free, I still had to pay around $1,200 just to fly from Sweden and stay at a hotel for three nights. And I travel cheap and alone. Six other families, each having between two and five members, were on the same bus from the Charles de Gaulle Airport in Paris, all heading to MineCon. You do the math; it was not a cheap trip for families.

In fact, it was not that cheap for Mojang either. MineCon is not a way for them to try to make more money. Not only had Lydia and Vu worked almost full-time with the event

Fans waiting for MineCon to begin. Thousands of people stood in line to get good seats for hours in the rain.

for several months, everyone at the office had been in Paris during the week to help set things up. Even though the visitors paid for the tickets, and Microsoft and Intel sponsored Mojang, they still were not able to meet the budget. They had to put in an extra $450,000 to make ends meet. One hundred and fifty thousand came from Markus's own pocket.

"We try telling people that MineCon is not a way for us to make money, but it's hard to get it across. Of course, it's an investment in Minecraft and our trademark, but it's most certainly not a source of income," says Carl.

Preparing for MineCon was less of an ordeal than the

first time, but a lot of energy still went in to it. There were thousands of details to take care of to get an event like this going. There are companies that make a living off arranging events such as this, which also indicates how big of a task MineCon is. That everything did not run smoothly should not come as a surprise. For example, the detailed information with schedules and maps was not published until the day before the event started. By then, most participants had already arrived at Disneyland.

It was Lydia who published the information, and she did so in the form of an app. She had done a massive job. But to have 7,000 people who had spent a lot of money on the event you invited them to, and not provide detailed information until the day before it all starts? In many other circumstances, that would have been considered an outrage. Not here though. I am sure some people were frustrated but I could not find them. Everyone seemed so full of expectations. This went to show two things: how far out on a limb Mojang goes when organizing something like MineCon and the level of devotion and trust the Minecraft community has for them.

I have read somewhere that as a journalist, you need to be cynical, and I guess this was where the cynic in me kicked in. Especially when Carl talked about this year's MineCon being about the fans and celebrating the community. The closer we got to the event, the more obvious it became that Mojang did not have any big news to share.

Not a very strange sight after an hour or two at MineCon. Fans of sports teams wear their colors; fans of Minecraft wear cartons on their heads. No weirder than that . . . or maybe a little.

They never intended to have a big release, like when Minecraft was officially released in Las Vegas. The plan was instead to release Scrolls in beta and for Markus to show something new from 0x10c, but once again Jakob and his team were too optimistic. The game was simply not good enough. And Markus, well, he had a hard time with the pressure building up.

"I got codeblock. I knew I had to make something to show at MineCon, but the last weeks I couldn't get anything done. Finally I just gave up," he says.

Apart from Lydia and Vu, Markus is the one at Mojang

who loves MineCon the most. That was why he helped pay for it with his own money. But that does not mean that it was an easy gig for the shy guy.

"No, I'm nervous weeks ahead. I'll never get used to or feel comfortable with the role I have at MineCon, being at the center of things. At the same time I step into that role, being Notch who made Minecraft. That makes the attention easier to handle than it normally would've been. If you are ever going to interview me, events like this is the time to do it, I'm already in character. I'm even rather comfortable with people taking pictures."

THAT THING WITH THE AUTOGRAPHS

In Las Vegas, there were scheduled times for the fans to get in line for autographs. It was a huge mistake. People stood in line for hours, yet many of them got nothing for it. There was just no way to get enough time for Markus, Jens and the others to meet the demand for their autographs. It seemed like every attendant wanted them to sign their names on a piece of paper or on Minecraft merchandise. The queuing system was frustrating for everyone, even for Markus and Jens who felt bad for the fans who got nothing. This year, it was handled differently. The fans would have to catch their idols as best as they could. All Mojangstas were encouraged to go out and interact with the fans as often as possible, but it was of course Markus and Jens who

Jens likes to look each person in the eyes before signing an autograph. It gets to be a lot of looking.

were the most coveted. Markus's plan was to take a walk or two in the event area and just roll with the flow.

"It's fun meeting the fans, and to be appreciated for a game I have made. But it's also hard for me. When you write autographs, you are very much at the center of attention. But the hardest part is that even if I do my best, I'll never be able to give it to everyone who wants it. I have to move on, but then there's always someone who doesn't get one and is disappointed. And then I feel guilty," he says.

Everything was complicated even further by the fact that the electro-house group Swedish House Mafia, one of

Markus's favorite bands, were doing their last concert in Sweden the night before MineCon started — and Markus had tickets. That was when being a multimillionaire came in handy. Markus's solution to the problem was to rent a private jet for him, Jakob and assistant Linn Hultman.

WORKING ALL NIGHT

No such luxury for yours truly, but there I was, a rainy morning at a deserted Disneyland. The night before, I spent a few hours with Jens, Carl, Vu and the others. It was chaotic. Nothing but the main stage seemed to be in order.

"It's no biggie, this is how it looks the day before a big event. You always have the feeling that there's no chance for things to be in order the next morning, but then, in some mysterious way, it always is," says Carl.

The others were not as convinced. Apart from the tent, there was also an exhibition center at Hotel New York. It was in utter chaos. When I arrived at Friday afternoon, I met Jens as I was to pick up my participant badge and the mandatory bracelet that would provide entry to MineCon. I asked him how things were going.

"It's a lot," he said.

Since it was the master of composure who was talking, I should have understood that those words really meant that it was more or less panic. Because one thing that Mojang had not counted on were the French contractors. The reports from Vu gave a clear image of many long breaks and not so much hard work. At 4 p.m. that Friday afternoon, the craftsmen had simply packed all their things and gone home, even though the exhibition halls, to be blunt, looked like crap. They had, of course, taken all the tools with them.

And there stood the 26 Mojangstas, about 20 hours before the opening of the event, with a half-finished MineCon in front of them. Since some of them had arrived the same day, Lydia and Vu were taking them all on a quick tour around the premises. I joined the tour, marveled at the chaos, was reassured by Carl that everything would be alright and went home at around eight. It turned out that most of the Mojangstas had kept working until 4 a.m., not as game developers but as handymen.

"It would've gone faster if we had had more tools. Any tools would have done, really. We only had one screw-driver," says Daniel.

The only one who seemed to be completely unaffected by the mess, who almost seemed energized by it, was Vu.

"I love this" was all he said, but quickly added that he had overestimated French work ethic.

I got the first sign of MineCon at Starbucks. There people were queuing for coffee all the way out on the shopping street that connected Hotel New York with the amusement park, where my hotel was. That was the first time I started wondering about what was in store for me that day. I have worked as a journalist for almost 30 years, in many different fields and at different places in the world. I have been to my fair share of press conferences, enormous and small-scaled ones. I have been to many E3s and other gaming conventions, sitting amongst thousands of journalists and fans that have been screaming loudly when Kinect has been shown, Nintendo 3DS revealed or the Super Mario creator Shigeru Miyamoto took to the stage. I have pushed and been pushed over to get a good picture or a quote. Carl and the others have also told me about MineCon in Las Vegas. I've read about it and seen pictures. I was trying to get a picture of it all in my mind.

But still. Despite all that, I was not prepared for what was waiting around the corner from Starbucks. There they were. Standing in a long row, probably over a thousand of them, maybe two thousand. The Minecraft fans. Mostly young boys. Some of them had cartons on their heads, cartons with holes for their eyes that made them look like the characters in the game. Others had dressed up completely, from top to bottom, some with blinking eyes, some so tightly wrapped in things that they could barely walk. Almost everyone was wearing the small black backpack given out at the check-in. It was over one hour until the gates opened, one and a half until the actual ceremony. It was drizzling and the air was chilly. But there they were. It was striking both how many of them there were, and how clean and well organized everything was. You might say well behaved.

When I met with Carl and we were walking along the line of people, which was growing by the minute, we were stopped several times. Fans were breaking out of the line to get an autograph from Mojang's CEO. It was really odd. I mean, the man does not even make any games. Carl himself just smiled.

"It's fun," he said. "It may have felt a bit weird the first few times, but now it's just fun."

MOJANGSTAMANIA

When it is time for the actual opening ceremony, the tent is packed. Around 7,000 people are there, including several versions of Steve and the Creeper. When Lydia is introduced and comes walking through the crowd in the spotlight, the crowd becomes loud, real loud. It may not be Beatlemania, but it is definitely not a standard welcoming for a community manager from a small game studio. It is obvious that Lydia loves being the center of attention. Carl and Markus do prefer to let Lydia take care of all public appearances, but it is also obvious that Lydia does not need much convincing. She enjoys herself when she greets all the fans. People scream, jump and wave things.

Then all the Mojangstas are introduced. They arrive in a long line, the same way Lydia came, walk up to the stage under the audience's deafening cheers. There should be 25 of them, but there are only 24. It is because Junkboy refuses to show his face in public. He also refuses to be in pictures. When he walked up on the stage in Las Vegas, he had one of those cartons on his head. Now he is lurking somewhere in the shadows at the back.

Because the stage is surrounded by seats, almost like a big boxing ring, they all have to walk up to Lydia, take the microphone and say who they are and what they do, then take a lap around the stage before leaving. It is in every way a strange scene. First of all, the audience, or maybe I should say the kids, cheer and scream. Then these idols. Twenty-five people who do not seem to have thought anything special of this day when they got dressed in the morning. It is the same jeans, T-shirts and shoes as any day at the office. They're not exactly oozing charisma and glamour from the stage. Historically, we journalists have been considered the worst dressed profession in Sweden, possibly beaten by the press photographers. But in all honesty, the Mojangstas are giving us a run for the money. The only one that seems dressed for the occasion is Lydia, which is not very surprising.

No one could care less though. And when finally Jens and then Markus enter the stage, the arena explodes. There is no doubt who the real stars are at Mojang. Jens belongs, according to himself, to those few Mojangstas who actually enjoy being onstage and Markus has entered his role as Notch. It is still striking how uncomfortable they are up there, despite all the love (that is the only way to describe it) that is declared to them from the fans.

As Markus heads from one part of MineCon to another, fans just follow him. Even though he's just headed for food. Sadly, this meant that Jakob Porser was left more or less alone in the main-stage tent when everyone left with Notch. At Markus's side is Linn.

A GURU AND HIS FOLLOWERS

One hour later, after the ceremony was over, all the Mojangstas gathered in a small greenroom where there would eventually be food served. Markus was happy, stood in front of the others and made his own version of a sexy belly dance with hands clasped behind his neck and challenging hip movements. It was by no means bad at all.

After a half hour, he left the room. The idea was to just stand close by and write some autographs for whoever happened to spot him. He had a bodyguard by his side, a really big Frenchmen. Linn was also there. Her job was to snatch hold of Markus when it got too much or when he had to leave. She was supposed to be the bad guy, the one who told the fans when Markus had to leave — even if they had not gotten their autograph. It worked pretty well.

Markus got almost five steps out of the door before he was forced to stop. A couple of fans close by saw him first, then the numbers quickly grew. In less than 10 minutes, it was almost like everyone had heard the rumors about Notch writing autographs. I was standing in the middle of everything trying to take pictures. The fans wanted autographs, to exchange a few words with their hero and then take pictures with him. At one point, he turned away and removed his snuff. Of course, many young and curious eyes were watching his movements and, of course, someone asked what he just did. Markus smiled shyly and answered that he uses nicotine and just removed it. Then he added: "Don't do that. It's bad. Nicotine is bad for you."

Almost like a big brother.

After a half hour, Linn did her thing and Markus said goodbye and went back into the greenroom again.

The idea was to go over to Hotel New York, where Mojang had a larger private room and where most things, apart from the bigger presentations, happened. But Markus and Linn quickly agreed that it was a bad idea; Markus was supposed to be on the big stage in less than an hour to be interviewed by Vu and then answer people's questions.

With all the fans waiting out there, he would have a hard time getting there and back in time.

It was once again almost fully seated in the tent when Markus walked up on the stage. Vu interviewed him and, with a half hour left, people were encouraged to stand in line behind a microphone if they wanted to ask Notch a question. It did not take many seconds before a long line, mostly consisting of young boys, formed. Some were so shy that they could barely say a word, but most of them were determined and each of them had a very specific question: If you could only learn how to use one software, what would it be? Was it hard to implement red stones in Minecraft? What is your best tip for becoming a game developer? Why are you wearing a hat?

Markus answered to the best of his ability, as one shy guy to another. When the 30 minutes were up, young boys were still standing in line for the microphone.

Then it was time for the next adventure, when Markus was to make his way from the tent to Hotel New York, nearly a 300-meter walk. The guard walked first and I had to jump in as assistant guard to hold the flank. It was necessary for Notch to be able to move forward at all. The first 50 meters, I had to hold my arm out and say "no, not now" to dozens of kids and youths who tried to stop our little cadre. Then something strange happened. It was like everyone understood that Markus would not stop. Instead, they all started walking behind him. When I ran a couple meters ahead to take pictures, I realized there was a long tail after Markus, it was surely a thousand fans walking there. Almost like Markus was a guru and they his disciples. Or perhaps like life on Twitter had suddenly been embodied; what happens every day in these youngsters' cellphones was now happening in real life. They were following Markus IRL.

It was a pretty sweet picture, especially since Markus was walking there holding his niece's hand. For Jakob and the people involved in Scrolls, the whole thing had a different consequence; they had the stage after Markus, but when they were about to begin, the tent was almost empty. Everyone followed Notch, just on the fly without having planned it.

JENS'S BIG DEBUT

MineCon was Jens's big coming-out party as lead designer for Minecraft. He was not as mobbed as Markus, but not far from it (by the way, Lydia's autograph was the third most coveted). At one point he had promised the fans to stand by the fountain outside Hotel New York at a certain time. I came with him and took pictures as the crowd kept growing around Jens, who patiently looked everyone in their eyes before writing his name.

A young man who held something out for him to sign said: "This must be really tough on you. You have to forgive us. Soon you'll be back at the office again." Jens nodded and answered that "yes, it's tough, but it'll be fine" and then "yes, it'll be nice to get back to the office."

It was so kind, polite and nice that it was a bit touching.

Markus had also noticed that Jens was more popular than ever amongst the fans.

"I had counted on it. But I thought that his popularity would take away some of the pressure from me. Instead it just seems to have become more on both of us. But I would probably get a bit jealous if the fans wanted his autograph more than mine, I have to admit that," he says.

It was not only the Mojangstas that were stars this weekend. YouTube celebrities were also attracting a lot of attention. At one point, CaptainSparklez was out walking (or he was trying to walk, but got stuck in the middle of a crowd) and attracted so much attention that people completely missed that Markus was walking past them. Even the visitors themselves had the opportunity to be temporary idols. The ones who had dressed up were constantly being photographed, even if they only had put a carton on their head.

JAKE GETS AN AUTOGRAPH

Inside the exhibition halls it was packed, of course. Every seat where you could play Minecraft was filled with kids and youths. The Cobalt and Scrolls computers were not attracting as many people, but Cobalt was more popular than Scrolls. It was not that strange, Scrolls takes awhile to get to know while Cobalt is easy to get started with. In the big tent, a few kids had hacked the computers so that they could play Minecraft on the Cobalt computers. It created merriness among the Mojangstas rather than anger: Of course the kids hack computers, ha, ha, they are so cute. Some of the parents stood or sat by the kids; others were more seasoned and set up camp in a corner with a book.

Out in the tent, the store Jinx was selling Minecraft clothes and merchandise. You had to stand in line for over an hour to buy something. When I got there on Sunday to buy something to bring home to my daughters, I saw a line that went through half the tent. I met Dick Haffner who brought his son, Jake, with him all the way from Maryland. Jake had a newly bought piece of carton on his head, while Dick had a bag in his hand. They had just waited in line for an hour and 15 minutes to be able to buy something.

"We usually play together, but only when we're alone. When Jake and his friends play, it gets too hard for me. I can't keep the pace," says Dick.

They had come to Paris solely for MineCon. Since they were here, they were to throw in a few days in Paris too. You might as well check out the Eiffel Tower, Notre Dame and the *Mona Lisa* while you were here. Jake had managed to get five autographs, not Markus's though. He spotted the badges around my neck through the carton, they were the same as everyone else's. Only, I had Notch's autograph on both of them. Not even the shadows from the carton could hide the sparkle in his eyes as he spotted them. I knew that Markus was not planning on going out to the fans anymore, it was pretty late on the Sunday. So I gave Jake one of my badges and in exchange I got to take a few pictures of him. I think he was smiling, but it was hard to tell. The carton was in the way. I never got to see his face.

WHO SAID THAT?

As far as I could tell, the two-day event ran smoothly to almost everyone's delight. Afterwards Carl noted that the visitors had been really pleased after Las Vegas, but that this time around they were extremely happy. The reviews and comments online were raving. The only incidents reported were: a sound engineer tried to squeeze more money out of Vu (he did not succeed, he did not have a gun); the wireless broadband in Mojang's private room did not get connected until there was only one hour of the event left (at that point everyone was too tired to even bother commenting about the French contractors and technicians); and a mother complained about something and wanted her money back (which she did get).

Markus handled the crowding and fame very well, and his alter ego Notch behaved well. Except once. At one point, someone got upset when he stopped signing autographs. This happened just outside Mojang's room at Hotel New York. When Markus opened the door to go inside, someone shouted "asshole" after him. It was a grown man's voice. Markus got pissed, turned around and walked out again. "Who said that?" he asked. Someone confessed and got scolded. "You don't act like that or use that language here, there will be no more autographs," said Markus and slammed the door after him.

Most people spent the Saturday evening riding carousels on one of the two amusement parks at Disneyland. Mojang had rented the whole place, so all the visitors got to ride for free. Personally, I had to sit for three hours to send pictures from the event to a photo agency. There was almost impressively slow Wi-Fi at my hotel.

For Markus's part, there was really only one thing missing. Red Bull. I have never heard a grown man ask for a beverage as much as he did during MineCon. It started on Saturday morning. He, Jakob and Linn arrived at Disneyland about the same time as the others finished with their drilling and nailing, around 4 a.m. When asked how he felt, he answered that all was well, although he needed some Red Bull. And this continued all through the event. "How the heck can they not have any Red Bull here?" became the big question. The truth is that they did have Red Bull, but at the kiosk by the train station right outside the gates. No one thought of checking there.

THEY DO NOT LOOK LIKE CELEBRITIES

On Sunday evening, it was time for Markus's party. The VIP tickets were distributed in black envelopes with a hat printed on them, Notch's signature. In the envelope, there was a black bracelet, also with a hat on it. Skrillex, maybe the world's hottest DJ, was going to be there. Markus rented Luc Besson's movie studio for the party. The only rule was that you couldn't go there by car, because there was nowhere to park it. I found out that Skrillex would perform sometime between 2 and 4 a.m. My first thought was that I am too old for this.

It was an impressive sight that met the partygoers when they arrived at the movie studio. Spotlights surrounded the enormous building and inside there was a sea of dancing people. Every MineCon visitor over 18 had gotten a free ticket. There were two up-and-coming DJs playing before Skrillex, but that did not seem to concern people this evening.

The VIP section turned out to be a raised area right behind the DJ booth. There were all the Mojangstas, their girlfriends plus a couple of hundred people. Alex Chapman was there, as well as the indie developer Mike Bithell who made such success with the game Thomas Was Alone during 2012. He got me a drink. It was an easy decision since Markus already had paid for everything. There were many more indie developers there, but I did not recognize anyone. Most of them were far from Notch's fame.

I was allowed to come to the party on one condition; I could not bring my camera. It sounded reasonable then, no one wants to be photographed late at night when the alcohol is free. But when Skrillex suddenly entered the stage, the condition seemed rather meaningless because almost everyone pulled out their smartphones to take pictures and film it. I did the same thing myself, trying to photograph the people taking pictures.

On the whole it was, of course, a very clean and well-behaved event. It was a bit like MineCon, but with alcohol. People were nice, happy, polite — and slightly drunk and dancing. When I was about to go to the VIP bathroom, I met a couple from Berlin. They had received tickets for having fixed something with the lighting, or maybe the sound, at MineCon. And they were a bit confused.

"I mean, this is a cool party and all, but we thought this was a VIP section," said the woman from Berlin.

"Oh yes, this is the VIP section," I replied.

"Oh, but . . . where are all the celebrities?" she then asked hesitantly.

I pointed at Jens, Markus, Patrick Geuder and some of the other visible Mojangstas. I pointed at Bithell and Chapman.

"Well, they don't look like celebrities," he said.

"Oh yes," I replied, "they are just a different kind of celebrities."

13
TAKING MINECRAFT TO SCHOOL

Not only do fans pay for both the ticket and trip to MineCon, many also contribute to the content of the convention. Throughout the weekend, panels are held in four or five different rooms, most of them led by some of the most prominent members of the community. A couple of the panels are about something called MinecraftEdu. That is Minecraft for schools.

For over a year, this special edition of Minecraft has been developed in Eastern Finland and in New York. Now it is polished and stable enough to be sold and marketed like a professional educational tool. This very unlikely cooperation between Eastern Finland and New York came about when two teachers, who at the time knew nothing of each other, came across Minecraft and realized its potential in the classroom. Since then, they have worked on what can best be described as an enormous mod with loads of special features.

"I honestly think that Minecraft has the power to change the way school in general views games. It can be such a powerful tool for educators that it may very well be the game that once and for all opens up the world of teaching to the power of gaming. I certainly hope so. Education needs it, teachers need it and, most of all, students need it," said Joel Levine.

There was no doubt about his passion. You could see that Joel was on a mission, a mission to change the way teaching is done. He talked fast, but that was only because he had a lot to say. "Just tell me when to stop, I can keep going for ever" were actually his first words when we met in New York. The hotel in Disneyland, I mean, not the actual New York where Joel is a grammar school computer teacher. He has had his current job at the private Columbia Grammar and Preparatory School at West 93rd Street for 10 years. He is also a gamer and has always tried to use video games in class.

"It's a thrilling way to get students engaged in learning, and it also makes them excited about coming to school," he said.

In the fall of 2010, he discovered Minecraft. The game was still in alpha, and still far from being the phenomenon it is today. Joel bought the game to play it himself. He found

When Joel Levine's daughter started learning math and spelling playing Minecraft, he knew he was on to something. He has introducing Minecraft as a tool for teaching in schools all over the world.

it both fun and engaging, but what really fascinated him was how his then five-year-old daughter interacted with it.

"I played it with her and was amazed at how much she was able to figure out and do in the game just by herself. She was solving problems and being self-reliant, but it went beyond just the game. She soon started to solve simple math problems, like calculating how many trees she needed to cut down to make certain things.

"She also learned to spell her very first word in the game. One day she came to me and asked how to spell *home*. She needed to know to be able to teleport herself to her home in the game. So I told her, and she went right to the computer and wrote her first word."

These experiences gave Joel the confidence to bring the game into his classroom. His original plan was to use it for a few weeks, and then just for basic computer skills. He designed a map where the students were supposed to type to each other rather than talk. He also wanted them to go to Minecraft wikis to find strategies for the game, because, as he put it, if they could use a Minecraft wiki, they could also use Wikipedia. But something completely different happened.

"Very soon they started to get into conflicts. One kid would break into another's home and steal things, someone would use unfriendly language and hurt other's feelings."

As the born educator and gamer he is, Joel did not take this as a sign of things going south. He made a different kind of lesson out of it instead.

"I quickly realized that this was an excellent tool to talk about how we behave in games and online. In my field of work we call it digital citizenship. It also includes things like what we make public and what we keep secret online. My school had been looking for ways to talk about these issues with the students at a younger age, since we had had some unpleasant experiences with online bullying with students in their teens. Minecraft turned out to be an excellent way to talk about these things."

That could have been the end to the story, if it had not

been for Joel blogging about it. Like so much else about Minecraft, the blog went viral. Soon, other teachers started talking about Joel's experiences with the game, newspapers got hold of the story and eventually students started getting in contact with Joel. They had mainly one question: How can we convince our teacher to use Minecraft? That was when he realized that he was on to something big.

Joel contacted Carl Manneh, and through him he got in contact with Santeri Koivisto, who was studying to become a teacher at the University of Joensuu in Eastern Finland and had made similar discoveries. Together they decided to start developing MinecraftEdu in a more professional way. They started a business in Finland and got working. That was in 2012, and like so much else in life, the project has taken more energy and time than Joel had thought. "I've learned more about international business and tax laws than I ever wished for," he says.

The business works like this: Joel and Santeri's company buys licenses at a reduced price from Mojang, and then sells them to schools. From that they are supposed to make a profit (if you would like more details, check out Minecraftedu.com). For Mojang, this project is not mainly about making money.

"Well, we're not losing money on it, but we're not doing it for the sake of making money either. On the other hand, being used in schools and played by students all over the world can never be bad for Minecraft," as Carl puts it.

However, one thing that Mojang is not interested in doing is taking care of the business aspect of it.

"No, we don't have time for that. We're not cut out for that kind of business anyway. We believe educators like Joel and Santeri handle it much better."

The only flaw with that plan is that Joel and Santeri are not salesmen — they are teachers. This may explain why it has been a rather slow process getting the mod ready. Still, even without really trying, they managed to sell MinecraftEdu to about 2,400 schools, and about 100 libraries, museums and other educational institutions are also using it.

"The mod hasn't really been stable enough to sell for use by teachers that are not computer teachers. But now we are ready to go into more of a marketing phase. It's rather exciting," says Joel.

FROM UR TO SPARTA

There are many features and tools that are unique to MinecraftEdu. For example, it is very easy to set up your own server, which is needed if an entire class is going to play together. You just push a button in the game and it is fixed, the same button that Jens and the others were trying to fix for the original Minecraft, the Minecraft Realms feature.

In MinecraftEdu there are tools for setting up boundaries for where on a map students can go, there are fast-building tools that allow the teacher to build with 10 blocks at a time and there is an easy teleportation system in the game for the teacher. You can also fast-save and quick-load maps.

"It must be as fast and simple as any [Microsoft] Office software. That's what ordinary teachers will expect, but it's also a much-needed feature. Often, you only have five minutes between classes, so being able to quickly save and load the game is essential."

Furthermore, the game has something called a freeze button. That is one of the first features Joel came up with for this edition of Minecraft. When the students got started with the game, he had a hard time getting their attention. They just would not listen to him, they could only focus on the game. Hence the freeze button. All you have to do is push it, and the game freezes for any number of students.

But in what kind of classes can Minecraft be used?

"Since you can do whatever you want in the game, it's basically limitless. You can use it for everything, math, geography, history, life sciences, anything," says Joel.

Joel opened up a map made by a teacher at an international school in Kuwait. It was enormous and had taken the teacher about 300 hours to build. It is now free to use for any other teacher who has MinecraftEdu. The map is used in history classes, and it covers everything from Roman villas to the first lighthouses. In some areas, the students are free to walk around but cannot interact with the game. In other places they are allowed to build for themselves.

For example, after visiting an area where they learn about the conflict between Athens and Sparta in ancient Greece, they go to a building area where they are given the task of building a training school for the famous Spartan warriors.

Not every map takes hundreds of hours to build, though. In California, sixth grade teacher Jeremy Biddle has built a map where his students are challenged to build Ur in Mesopotamia, one of the first cities in the world. In the game they are faced with the same challenges as the first citizens of Ur were facing, or at least the Minecraft version of them. Among other things, Biddle rebuilt the famous Ziggurat, the temple of Ur. It took him 10 hours.

SCHOOL IS FUN AGAIN

Even though many teachers have already embraced Minecraft and other computer games as educational tools, there are a lot of skeptics out there. Even at Columbia Grammar and Preparatory School.

"In the beginning there were a few teachers at my school who were not convinced using Minecraft was a good thing. But I got them into my classroom and after five minutes they had changed their minds. That's what happens. If you just can get the skeptics into the classroom for five minutes, they are generally convinced," says Joel.

The same goes for parents.

"I've had some parents that were concerned about using

video games in class. I dealt with them the same way I dealt with my colleagues, I invited them to class. And the same thing happened; they saw with their own eyes how good it was. The response has been everything from parents being happy that their kids love going to school again to being glad the kids are playing a non-violent video game."

Joel had also built his own new maps. For Earth Day in April, he created an adventure map for his third graders. In the game, the students wake up in a cave. Once they get out of the cave, they discover that they are the only survivors after a natural disaster caused by global warming. Searching the island together, they find clues to both the story behind the catastrophe and what they are supposed to do. As it turns out, they are not really on an island, but on top of the Himalayas. That is the only part of earth that is not covered by water. In another cave, they find the only surviving tree. They are given a dual mission: kick-start the ecology and send a rocket to space. The rocket is a signal for the other survivors that they can return, which they only can do after a hundred trees have been planted (that is when, in this game, the ecology is started).

"But here's the thing, the two goals are at odds with each other. They need to get iron and then smelt it, but in order to smelt it they need wood. So they both need to plant trees, and cut them down. There is a conflict, and the students need to discuss it and find a balance. In reality it becomes a discussion of the conflict between development and nature, between production and global warming. It's a very serious matter, but in a Minecraft setting it becomes fun and engaging. Most of all, the students learn a lot," said Joel.

There are numbers of examples like this online, and in Joel's inbox there were numerous emails from principals, teachers and students that are testimonies to what MinecraftEdu can contribute to education. There was, for example, the principal who was at first skeptical to the idea of MinecraftEdu, then allowed a teacher to use it, witnessed the success and now encouraged all teachers to get involved. What makes Joel the happiest is when students or parents email him. There were students who thanked him for making school fun again and parents telling him that their kid used to hate school but now could not get enough of it.

"Games have something that is very hard to teach students. It's that intangible thing that makes you go at a problem again and again, from different angles. To a gamer that is natural, that is how you play games. Yet that is not how we typically do it in school," he says.

"In school it is still very much the old trick with study, study, test and then study, study, test again. You get one shot at it, and then it's over. That structure and way of teaching and learning is making less and less sense in the modern world. That's why students dropping out of school are such a growing problem in the world. My earnest belief is that using games in education can change that trend. And Minecraft is the best tool for it right now."

If MinecraftEdu was to change the way people behave online, maybe it would also solve Markus's problem with the haters on Twitter. He has his own take on digital citizenship.

"It would make sense with those kinds of lessons, really. But maybe not a lesson about online etiquette, but a lesson that makes you understand that everyone on the internet is human, just like you. That everything you say and do has consequences. Be mean if you want, but be aware that you are being mean to real people."

14
ANOTHER
15,000 REASONS
TO BE HAPPY

The weekend before Christmas 2012, Carl, Markus, Daniel Kaplan and Linn Hultman visited Glasgow to celebrate together with 4J Studios. 4J had struck gold when they got to work with Mojang, because in the deal they got their share of the profit off the Xbox sales. With five million copies sold, their life as a small game studio in Scotland had become a lot more stable.

A few days later, Mojang had their combined Christmas dinner and Christmas party. That was when that year's bonuses were revealed. It ended up being $15,000 per person, after taxes. That amounts to about four months' pay each. It cost Mojang almost a million dollars. No one was tweeting.

The $15,000 each may not have felt all that much when Mojang as a whole was moving towards a turnover of about

$220 million U.S. with a profit in the neighborhood of $85 million. The lack of tweets could also have been because of the money they all received earlier that year, maybe this did not seem, on the whole, that big a deal?

"I was prepared for some sort of bonus. Last year we got one month's extra pay; this year it was a lot more. Fifteen thousand dollars is a lot of money," said Jens.

He was, of course, happy and grateful, but also a bit concerned.

"It's like the money I got in February, it's extra money, nothing you can count on. If you're going to be given bonuses on a regular basis, you would like to know how they are going to be calculated. You want to know how much money you have to spend."

But Jens, on the other hand, had also managed to increase his pay significantly during the year.

"I realized that it's not always how you perform that gives you a higher salary; what you say in the salary negotiation can be even more important. So I started out with a very high number and then we negotiated it down to about the level I wanted to be at. So I'm pleased," he said.

There was also the old indie thoughts that kept popping up in his mind.

"Yes, there is something nagging at me sometimes. As an indie, I and the ones I worked with always had the mindset that it is the one who works on a game that gets the money it makes. But that's not how it works here at

Mojang, and I guess it couldn't work like that either. It's not what I make in Minecraft that generates money, it's the game itself, you could almost say the brand, which was made by Markus."

The issue has also been discussed by the board, meaning over a dinner with Markus, Jakob and Carl.

"To calculate bonus systems in our situation is really, really hard. How do you do that when some people work with Minecraft and others with Scrolls, for example? One game generated millions in revenue [in] 2012, the other nothing," says Carl.

The three owners have set another goal instead: they simply aim at being the best workplace — in the world.

"It's about everything really, from being fun to work for us and that we should work with fun things that we are passionate about, to us paying for trips, arranging exciting stuff and give great bonuses and gifts. We probably won't come up with a system for it, I don't even know if we want to."

And about that indie thing?

"You cannot compare us to other indie developers in that way. If you compare us to any other, regular company instead, it is incredibly generous to give four months' salary as a bonus to every employee. It doesn't happen anywhere but here I think."

The Christmas party itself seemed to have been held in just that spirit, the world's funnest company spirit that is. Markus did not show up for the interview we had

Carl Manneh's goal as CEO of Mojang is not just to create a nice working environment, but to make it the best place to work in the world.

scheduled the next day, and it was very unusual that he missed an appointment in that way. Linn thought that he might be hungover. Markus sent an email, apologized and explained that he was indeed hungover, but that he had had to stay up all night with a friend who was having some relationship problems.

I also noticed that I myself had become slightly desensitized over the year. Fifteen thousand dollars did not sound like a lot of money to me either anymore. Not that I am a rich man by any means, but I had simply gotten used to high numbers and Hollywood producers. When Carl mentioned that he had gotten access to Skype founder and fellow Swede Niklas Zennström's business network, which is a big deal, I did not even react. When he told me that Markus had paid $150,000 out of his own pocket to ensure that MineCon happened, I forgot to take notes on it. It simply did not seem that big of a deal.

When Carl interrupted the interview in May and told me about the sale numbers on Xbox Live, I was impressed. When Markus, on Christmas Day from Thailand, tweeted that Minecraft sold 453,000 copies that day, I barely reacted, even though he ended it with a "wowers!" (Even Markus seemed to have gotten a bit numb, the happiness did not last long even in Thailand. Right after the "wowers" he tweeted: "And immediately after tweeting that, my food arrived late and wrong. Oh, the rollercoaster of emotions!" Who said that life is easy just because you are a multimillionaire?)

The 435,000 copies meant some $6 million on Mojang's accounts, Carl told me over the phone the day before New Year's Eve. The numbers were staggering. But even Carl felt that he had become blind to numbers.

"Of course you get numb. I'm almost never surprised anymore. I understand that what's happening is unusual and very special, but very rarely something surprises me," he said.

It is not just the money and everything that happens around Mojang I had gotten used to; even Carl's and all of

Mojang's honesty and openness was becoming something I was getting very used to. Maybe I did not take it for granted, but I would have been very surprised if Carl, Markus, Jakob or anyone else did not want to answer my questions, even if they were a bit delicate. Carl did not even get defensive when I asked him if giving out bonuses without a system eventually could be viewed as handouts, or when I said that $15,000 on one hand is a lot but, on the other, little compared to Mojang's profits. He reasoned about it and explained how he and the others thought instead. If things are complicated, then that is what he says. That is, for me, perhaps the real greatness in what has happened, and is happening, in front of my eyes with Mojang throughout the year. Something that is truly unique, and something that also says a lot about Markus. All that talk about everyone having to think and say what they want is not just talk. It is a motto he believes in and lives by.

This book is written almost in the face of Mojang, I do not claim to have much of a distance to anything happening. On the contrary. I have done my best to be as close to them as ever possible. To have a distance from Mojang was never the goal of this adventure; I simply realized that Mojang was in the middle of something unique and of historical importance and I wanted to chronicle it as best I could. My ambition has been to be in the middle of it all, and try to get to know the company and its main characters as well as possible. I do not know if I have succeeded, though Carl's first comment after proofreading was that "this is a book I want to read in 20 years just to remember how things were," which I guess is as good a review as I could have hoped for.

I did not realize it myself, but after getting feedback from other people reading through this book, I can see that Markus, Carl and the others are portrayed in a rather favorable way. It is almost like a love story. Teenagers that have read through it want to work at Mojang, and adults are thrilled by the chapters on UN and education. That has not been my goal at all; but on the other hand, I have merely tried to tell things as they are, or at least seem to be. I have asked a lot of questions, even hard and intimate ones, and the answers I have been given are the ones you have read. I do not think that Mojang or the Mojangstas are without fault, but as far as I can tell they are very nice people in a position — because of the riches that Minecraft pull in — to work in a pace and space that few of us are.

If I have one worry about the future, it might be just that: What will the money do to them? Can Markus remain the same in, say, five or 10 years? Can he still be passionate about making games and changing the gaming industry while being ridiculously rich? And what happens when — because it always does — some kind of backlash comes, when maybe the love of the community is tested?

But this is not really the time and place to foretell the future, at least not more than the most imminent one.

I mean, as you read this, the future is already here. As of December 2013, Scrolls has been released in beta and has over 110,000 players; Minecraft Realms is also out in beta and more gamers will be let in over time. Markus is no longer focused on 0x10c, but outside Mojang it's still being worked on. And somewhere in Hollywood, agents are still trying to sell the idea of a Minecraft movie. Minecraft Xbox edition has been released as a retail version — the old-school way as a disc in a box — and has hit the top ten all over Europe and in the USA.

A new Xbox One edition has been announced by Microsoft, and Sony finally revealed that PlayStation would also get its own version. New Minecraft Lego sets hit stores, and Danish publishing house Egmont released beginner guidebooks for kids designed in part by Junkboy — and promptly had to print a million copies, according to GamesIndusty.

In April 2013, Markus and Jens were astonished to find out they'd been included on *Time* magazine's list of the world's most influential people. When the news arrived at the studio, no one was really prepared for it.

"So much is happening all the time that I am seldom caught off guard, but this was something out of the ordinary even for us. At first we did not understand what it was, it was totally unexpected," said Carl when I interviewed him for story about the news.

Markus opted to stay home and skip *Time*'s gala event.

Going to a big dinner party with celebrities, a red carpet and tons of journalists is just not his cup of tea. Instead Jens went with Carl. Unfortunately, the celebration in New York happened to coincide with a planned visit from Sweden's Prince Daniel, which then had to be rescheduled.

In February, I was able to break the news of Mojang's staggering profit: a whopping $92 million before tax. Mojang turned over $237 million. The story went viral within minutes as it was picked up internationally; Notch even arranged to answer questions about being rich on the popular online forum Reddit. As always, he did so very frankly and honestly. Not only was Markus one of Sweden's richest people after 2012, he also was paying a lot of taxes, fourth most in the country as it turned out.

During the spring of 2013, Mojang also managed to bring all their employees on a trip to Monte Carlo in private jets, with rented luxury sports car waiting at the airport and a private concert with the Norwegian electronic music duo Röjksopp. And, finally, when the 7,000 tickets for MineCon 2013 in Orlando were released in three blocks, they sold out in less than 10 seconds. The list of 2013's accomplishments for the company goes on and on; nothing with Minecraft got smaller or lesser. When the world's first opera made in Minecraft and performed by live singers was streamed in December, it was barely noticed — even though it was something truly extraordinary.

And even though Minecraft has sold more than 20

million copies across all platforms, so far Mojang has really only been able to sell the PC edition of the game in a good way in a handful of countries. Minecraft still has an ugly website with a payment solution that does not even work in countries such as Brazil and Poland, to take two countries where many are playing the free version of the game, but very few have been able to buy it. At the time of writing, Mojang is working with Japan and Korea to find ways to make Minecraft more available there. And as Minecraft Realms is finally being released, new ways of earning money on a monthly basis open up to Mojang. In interviews about Realms, Carl Manneh has insisted to me that Realms, in the end, has the potential to bring larger revenue for Mojang than Minecraft itself.

As for me, there is only one conclusion I can safely make: it is very hard to predict anything about the future of Mojang and Minecraft. They will continue to try their hardest to be the world's best workplace, they will try to be just as open with everything as they always have been, and they will make tons of money.

Maybe that is good enough for now?